After October 7

Rabbi Menachem Creditor

After October 7

2024 Paperback Edition, *First Printing*
© 2024 Menachem Creditor

ISBN: 9798341451902

In memory of Hersh z"l.

For Am Yisrael.

*With gratitude to the UJA-Federation of New York
family of staff, donors, and volunteer leaders,
a beautiful army of angels helping to lift up
the Jewish People, New York, and the whole world.*

"We are living in difficult and dark times. I can't seem to shake off the sense that we have returned to Jewish history, to saying *"b'chol dor vador"*—from generation to generation—they rise up against us. And I can't keep from crying out in frustration and horror at this phrase's taste of truth. We are facing multiple battles in Israel, in America, and around the world. The most important weapon at our disposal, the one we have to nourish and insist upon, is peoplehood—feeling and behaving as one being."

- Mijal Bitton, *That Pain You're Feeling Is Peoplehood* (Sapir Journal, November 2, 2023)

also published by Rabbi Menachem Creditor:

Crackling and Alive

These Holy Days: A High Holiday Supplement After October 7
co-edited with Dr. Ora Horn Prouser

A Difficult Beginning: A Post October 7 Commentary on the Book of Genesis
co-edited with Daphne Lazar Price

God Kisses: Selected Writings 2023

Israel Poems

Calling Out: Psalms for Today
co-edited with Sarah Tuttle-Singer

Seder Interrupted: A Post-October 7 Hagaddah Supplement
co-edited with Dr. Ora Horn Prouser

To Write of Love During War: Poems

Am Yisrael Chai: Essays, Prayers, and Poems (Volumes One and Two)

The Consequences of Listening: Selected Writings 2018-2022

Impossible Torah: The Complete AI Torah Commentary

Ending Gun Violence: Essays, Prayers, and Poems

All Who Can Protest: A Rabbinic Call to End the American Gun Violence Epidemic
co-edited with Rabbi Rachel Timoner, Rabbi Isaiah Rothstein, and Rabbi Michelle Dardashti

Honey from the Rock: A Pandemic-Era Rabbinic Anthology

Jewish Resilience: Rabbinic Reflections After Colleyville

A Year of Torah

Fault Lines: Exploring the complicated place of Progressive American Jewish Zionism
co-edited with Amanda Berman

A Rabbi's Heart

Remember and Do Not Forget
co-edited with Rabbi Jesse Olitzky

When We Turned Within: Reflections on COVID-19, Volumes 1 & 2
co-edited with Sarah Tuttle-Singer

Loud, Proud, and Jewish

Open to Wonder: Selected Writings (2015-2017)

None Shall Make Them Afraid: A Rabbis Against Gun Violence Anthology

Holding Fast: Jews Respond to American Gun Violence

To Banish Darkness: Modern Reflections on Hanukkah

yes, my child: poems

Intense Beginnings (Selected Writings 2014)

What Does it Mean? (Selected Writings 2006-2013)

The ShefaNetwork Archive

Not By Might: Channeling the power of Faith to End Gun Violence

And Yet We Love: Poems

Primal Prayers: Spiritual Responses to a Real World

The Hope: American Jewish Voices in Support of Israel

Siddur Tov LeHodot (Shabbat Morning Transliterated Prayerbook)

Peace in Our Cities: Rabbis Against Gun Violence

Commanded to Live: One Rabbi's Reflections on Gun Violence

Slavery, Freedom, and Everything Between: The Why, How and What of Passover
co-edited with Rabbi Aaron Alexander

Thanksgiving Torah: Jewish Reflections on an American Holiday

AFTER OCTOBER 7

CONTENTS

Essays

HOLIDAYS

INTRODUCTION

One Year After October 7:
We Will Not Be Broken

We stand – right now – in the liminal space between Rosh Hashanah and Yom Kippur, the Days of Awe. Tomorrow marks the first anniversary of one of the darkest days in Jewish history: October 7, 2023. On that day, Israel endured a brutal and devastating attack that shattered lives, altered families, and pierced the heart of our people. It was not just an attack on Israel; it was an attack on all Jews everywhere. And the wave of Antisemitism that has grown since then has been relentless. For many, this past year has been a harsh reminder of the dangers we face simply for being Jewish.

Yet, in the face of this, we must remember the core truth of our people: Am Yisrael Chai—the people of Israel live! We are still here. We have faced destruction before, we have mourned our losses, and each time, we have rebuilt. Our very survival is an act of defiance. Our resilience is a sacred inheritance. From generation to generation, we have been charged with carrying the flame of Jewish life, and even now, amidst the grief and fear, we carry it forward.

As we approach Yom Kippur, we are asked to look inward, to reflect on who we are and who we want to be. But this year, as we stand one year after the murders of so many Jews, our sisters and brothers and babies and parents and grandparents - in ways that rival the worst our People has ever experienced, our reflection must go beyond personal introspection. This year calls for something greater: a collective reawakening. We are called to stand together, to reclaim our Jewish pride, and to support each other as never before.

Our young Jews on college campuses, in particular, need us now. They are facing a surge of antisemitism in environments that often feel hostile to their very identity. It is our responsibility to protect them, to let them know that they are not alone, and to remind them of the strength they come from. We must show up for them in real ways—by speaking out, by educating others, by creating spaces of safety and belonging. We cannot abandon them to fear or alienation. They are the present and future of our people, and they must know that we stand with them, that we are proud of them, and that they are part of something ancient, strong, and enduring. And worthy. *And beautiful.*

This is not a time for us to shrink back or hide our identity. This is a time for us to stand tall as Jews, with pride in who we are and where we come from. For thousands of years, we have endured persecution, and yet we have never allowed the hatred of others to define us. We have always defined ourselves—by our commitment to justice, to learning, to family, to community. This is what it means to be Jewish. And now, in this difficult moment, we must reclaim that identity with even greater passion. We must hold our heads high and remind the world—and ourselves—that we are a people of strength, of resilience, of hope.

Tomorrow, as we mark the anniversary of the attack, let it be a day not only of raw mourning but of decisive resolve. Let it be a day when we recommit to one another, to our people, to our homeland the State of Israel, and to our values. Let it be a day when we say: We will not be broken. Our enemies have tried for generations to destroy us, but we are still here. And we will continue to be here, thriving, forever.

We are one people, no matter where we live, no matter our backgrounds. Whether in Israel, on campuses, in cities around the world, we are part of one unbreakable, shimmering chain. We must protect one another. We must fight for one another. We must love one another with the depth and fierceness that our history demands and that our descendants deserve.

As Yom Kippur approaches, we prepare to stand before God and each other, humbled but unafraid. The words of the *Unetaneh Tokef*—"Who shall live and who shall die"—have taken on new meaning this year. We have been reminded all too well the fragility of life and the cost of hatred. But we also remember the power of life, the strength of our traditions, and the indomitable spirit of our People.

So let us march into Yom Kippur – and beyond – not only seeking forgiveness, but renewing our commitment to a strong and vibrant Jewish future. Let us hold our heads high with Jewish pride. Let us support our children with unwavering love and solidarity. And let us continue to show the world, as we have for millennia, that no force on Earth can extinguish the flame of Jewish Life.

G'mar Chatimah Tovah. May we all be written and sealed for a future of strength, unity, and pride.

4 Tishrei 5785
October 7, 2024

12

Book Introductions

Introduction to Am Yisrael Chai, Vol. 1

I can't write this introduction. I don't want to. It was never meant to be written. Just like this book was never meant to be created. It just hurts so much.

Am Yisrael Chai is an emergency response anthology of voices from all over the world, grieving and writhing from the horrors perpetrated upon the State of Israel on Simchat Torah 5784, October 7, 2023, when thousands of Hamas terrorists, may their names and memories be forever erased, breached the borders of the State of Israel and massacred over 1,300 people, slaughtering them in cold blood, rooms of infants, grandparents, entire families burnt to death, and scores of young people at a music festival celebrating peace. More than 3,000 have been severely injured. More than 200 people, including infants and Holocaust Survivors, were stolen from their homes and taken hostage in Gaza by Hamas. The terrorists documented their craven acts, often on their victims' phones, and sent them to their families. Unfathomably terrible images are now forever emblazoned in our eyes, spread through social media where children have seen them as well.

The entire Jewish world is in trauma. And while the Jewish community has mobilized hundreds of thousands at countless vigils and rallies in support of Israel, there are also well-attended rallies on American campuses and in the streets of places like Morocco and London - *cheering on Hamas.*

This was not Poland in 1942. It was 9 days ago in my homeland, the Third Jewish Commonwealth, *Medinat Yisrael*, the State of Israel. I have never compared anything to the *Shoah*, but I do today. The scope and scale of the evil defies any other comparison.

What happened in the State of Israel was a massive Pogrom, a term that was supposed to be consigned to history, a warning from the past invoking ancestral martyrs for the sake of a safer future. It was not supposed to be part of the lived experience of Jewish children.

My trembling fingers are trying not to continue typing. I cannot breathe. My heart is stopped. I cannot fathom what I have just written. Which is why an anthology like this is so necessary, however terrible its subject.

We bear witness. We must.

As I write, my beloved brother in Israel is on his way with Israeli journalists to *Kibbutz Be'eri*, in the south of Israel, near the border with Gaza. It was the sight of mass murder. I desperately do not want him to go. But go he must. And he carries us all with him into the nightmare, just as we all, Jews around the world, are in this together, ravaged heart to ravaged heart, torn soul to torn soul.

Debra A. Fisher, a daughter of a Shoah survivor tells the story of how she begged her father to tell her what he experienced in the Holocaust.[1] All her life he held it from her. Upon his deathbed, as she pressed him to tell her, he becomes angry and says,

> "It's like since you were a little girl, you've been banging on this door in a room that I'm in all by myself. You keep saying, 'Daddy, let me in this room! Let me in the room!' And I keep saying, 'Go away! You cannot come in here!' ...If I open this door and I let you in this room, you will never be able to leave this room. You'll be in this room forever. It will be a nightmare you cannot get rid of. You will wake up to it, and you will go to sleep with it. That's what's in this room, and I do not want to open that door for you."

To this, Debra responds:

> "But, Dad, I need for you to. *I just need to know.*"

She reflects on what she heard from her father:

> "The images that he painted for me in that room, what happened to him and his brothers and others around him, they were so horrific. I felt a part of me die. And slowly I realized that he was right: Once you enter that room, you cannot leave. I am in that room when I sleep and when I wake. It's always with me."

This is a book of horrific testimony, dear friends. Images and recollection, response and prayer, all of it generated because we are in this very sad room together.

That's why the collection bears the title *Am Yisrael Chai*. This is our life – and we share it, recommitting to life itself, fighting for it,

---

[1] recorded in David Isay's *Listening is an Act of Love, p. 174-176*

praying for it. We have always known that hateful people have targeted Jews throughout time, and we thought we had changed their impact on our history because we had finally come home. We'd become a new kind of Jew. And we have. We've created a powerful homeland, complicated and imperfect, infuriating and exalting, pride- and cringe- inducing, normal and exceptional. We changed, in profound ways.

We changed. But the Simchat Torah Pogrom of 2023 tells us that the world has not. Not yet.

And we are now in this room together, when we sleep and when we wake, when we are at home and on our ways.

In the immediate aftermath of trauma, one cannot be expected to be thoughtful, mindful, creative. And yet you hold a collection of soulful and eloquent expressions of pain and Global Jewish Solidarity make the choice of title for this collection even more clear, and emphatic: *Am Yisrael Chai!*

I couldn't be more grateful to the many, many authors who sent in their heart's expressions to this project. Thank you for your raw, passionate, pulsing souls.

Every weekday we pray:

שׁוֹמֵר יִשְׂרָאֵל
שְׁמוֹר שְׁאֵרִית יִשְׂרָאֵל
וְאַל יֹאבַד יִשְׂרָאֵל
הָאֹמְרִים שְׁמַע יִשְׂרָאֵל

Guardian of Israel,
guard the remnant of Israel,
and let not Israel perish,
we are the ones who say, "Hear O Israel."

Never in my life have I understood these words so well, felt them so acutely. The breach in Israel's defense and the premeditated murder of thousands of my family members has shaken my sense of things. As the great Elie Wiesel once wrote, "As a Jew, I need Israel. More precisely, I can live as a Jew outside Israel but not without Israel." Never again will we see the world the same. Never again.

As of the moment this manuscript went to print, a mere 9 days after the atrocity that struck our people in the heart, UJA-Federation of New York has raised over 85 million dollars from donors in support of our Emergency Israel Campaign, and we have already allocated 22 million of it to organizations on the ground in Israel who are supporting those in harm's way, those in dire need, and those who have lost family members. We are there in a profound way, to help our People in this dark time. All proceeds from this book project will support UJA-Federation of NY's Emergency Israel Campaign.

We will never bring back those whose lives we have lost. There are too many new stars in the sky. But we lift up our eyes to Heaven and we will remember them as a blessing. We will, as our hearts regain strength, heal that which has been broken. But we will never, not ever, be the same.

May this collection be of real support to our sisters and brothers, our parents, our grandparents, and most of all - our children.

May the Holy One bless *Medinat Yisrael*, the State of Israel, *Reisheet Tz'michat Ge'ulateinu*, the beginning of the flourishing of our redemption.

May our family see better days very, very soon.

Am Yisrael Chai!

Rosh Chodesh Mar Cheshvan, 5784
October 16, 2023

Introduction to Am Yisrael Chai, Vol. 2

> "I cannot help withstanding evil when I see that it is about to destroy the good. I am forced to withstand the evil in the world, just as I withstand the evil within myself. I can only strive not to have to do so by force. I do not want force. But if there is no other way of preventing the evil destroying the good, I trust I shall use force and give myself up into God's hands."
>
> -Martin Buber, *A Land of Two Peoples*

This is not quite an introduction. I couldn't write one. In fact, the contents of this volume have been in place for some time, but I just couldn't bring myself to craft anything like an introduction. How could I possibly frame a second book of Essays, Poems, and Prayers in response to the horrors of October 7, 2023?

Am Yisrael Chai, Book One was published on October 17, 2023, just as I and 28 other New York rabbinic leaders journeyed to Israel on a UJA-Federation of New York Solidarity Mission. Standing closer to the immense pain of our People proved the axiom that proximity is power. The physical and psychic aches defy description, and my every attempt at language points directly at things I can barely acknowledge.

So, Dear Reader, I apologize. These thought-fragments that follow are the best I can do. I hope they do justice to the contributions of so many caring and thoughtful authors who words fill the pages of this book of scarred and sacred testimony.

Though as I write these words, tonight is the fifth night of Channukah, it is somehow still October 7. Though so much has transpired in these harsh 67 days, it is also still that ravaging day.

Early that Shabbat morning, which was also Simchat Torah, 3,000 rockets and thousands of Hamas terrorists invaded the State of Israel, murdering over 1,200 people including hundreds of young adults at the Super Nova music festival. They stole 250 Israeli babies, children, parents, grandparents, and Holocaust survivors from their homes. Jews, Muslims, and Christians from 33 countries were also among the hostages. Jewish, Arab, and Druze Israelis were butchered by Hamas.

Terrorists committed brutal sexual violence against women and atrocities against babies, massacring families in front of each other and laying waste to entire communities of civilians, all the while filming their acts on their GoPro recording devices and also livestreaming their attack on the social media feeds of their victims' cellphones.

Writing these words feels surreal. This cannot have happened. I must be in the middle of a nightmare. It cannot be true. But on November 28, my second solidarity mission to Israel after October 7, I visited Kibbutz Kfar Aza, the site of one of the massacres. I wrote that day:

> There simply aren't words to name what happened, the horrific scent in the air, the pain. I've always pushed against Shoah comparisons, but they are the only ones that come to my heart. This was never supposed to happen in our home. It was never supposed to happen again. I know that the great work of national rebirth is underway with full force, that the Jewish People is unified in a way we haven't been for so long, that we will rebuild. But right now my soul is reeling.

I will never unsee what I saw nor unsmell what I smelled. I will always be staring at the burnt mezuzah with the sacred acronym *Shadai* for *"Shomer Delatot Yisrael/Guardian of the Doorways of Israel"* at the entry to what had been a family's precious home. But my intense feeling, as someone who visited the scorched earth and displaced survivors, but did not, thank God, experience this myself, cannot compare to the actual experience of countless others.

We must be prepared to stand witness to all of this horror. We must, because despite all of the testimony, the horrific recordings by the wretched terrorists (may their memories be obliterated from under Heaven), bullet holes beyond counting, too much blood staining countless floors, and body parts entangled in shells of burnt-out cars and bomb shelters, there are many around the world who have already declared that there was no assault, or that October 7 must be contextualized, or that it was somehow deserved. The global gaslighting of the Jews has barreled ahead full steam.

On college campuses all over the United States, anti-Israel student groups advertised a "Day of Resistance" on October 12 with ads featuring images of the Hamas paragliders used in the terror attack. And two months later, the Presidents of MIT, Harvard, and UPenn testified to Congress on December 5 that calls by student groups on campus for Genocide against Jews only violate the standards of their institutions in certain contexts.

These are blasphemous denials of the human rights of Jews, willingly enabled in American halls of higher education. Jewish college students have been confronted with dehumanization by faculty members and peers with chants of eradication that harken back to horrific chapters of Jewish history.

On October 13, the United Nations Entity for Gender Equality and the Empowerment of Women issued a statement equating Hamas's terror with Israel's military response, failing to even mention the terror group by name or address its sexual assaults.

Let it be shouted, written, sworn, etched in stone:

There is no context for rape of Jewish women.
There is no context for placing Jewish infants in ovens.
There is no context for families being burnt alive.
There is no context for genocide against Jews.

We must name what happened. We must. As Senator Kirsten Gillibrand said during a protest of the UN's silence:

> "It's important that we are giving a voice to the women raped and murdered on October 7, and it is important that we are speaking truth to power in this place at this time. ... The horrific acts by Hamas are indescribable, I've seen much of the raw footage. The sheer level of evil, you can't unsee it; it haunts you. While it is hard to tell these stories, we must collectively ensure

that the world knows the heinous, barbaric nature of Hamas. We must ensure this is engraved in history for all time."

And even more piercingly, as Ayelet Levy Shachar, mother of Naama Levy, wrote:

> You have seen the video of my daughter Naama Levy. Everyone has. You have seen her dragged by her long brown hair from the back of a Jeep at gunpoint, somewhere in Gaza, her gray sweatpants covered in blood. ... On October 7, Naama had been sleeping at Kibbutz Nahal Oz, and was awakened by the chaotic sound of a missile barrage. At 7 a.m., she sent me a WhatsApp message: "We're in the safe room. I've never heard anything like this." That was the last I heard from her. ...There are seventeen young women still in captivity. They range in age from 18 to 26. I think of what they, and my Naama, could be subjected to at every moment of the day. Each minute is an eternity in hell. ...The seventeen female hostages are not bargaining chips to be debated by diplomats. They are daughters, and one of them is mine. My primal scream should be the scream of mothers everywhere. Bring her home now![2]

They are daughters. They are our daughters. Our screams must continue until they are home in our arms.

In the face of the greatest massacre of Jews since the Shoah, I have been incessantly confronted by those who wonder where my grief is for Palestinian civilians. I've been asked terribly offensive questions like, "Do you only cry for Israeli babies?"

My response:

When one visits a shiva home, do we ask the mourner if they also grieve for their neighbor's losses? Of course not. We know their wounded hearts have the capacity for empathy, but we honor the mourner's pain by being humble and understanding as they grieve. My People's children have been murdered, parents have been brutalized, grandparents massacred, and my family is being held hostage.

---

[2] Ayelet Levy Shachar, *"The Woman in the Hamas Video Is My Daughter"*, The Free Fress, December 8, 2023

Expecting anything other than primal grief for our unfathomable loss is to deny Jews the right to feel the excruciating intimacy of family and to rob us of our family's dignity.

We are witness to the erasure of Jewish pain and dignity by countless others.

In the course of war, especially given Hamas' strategy of placing civilians in harm's way, any action Israel's Defense Forces takes leads to horrific civilian losses. But imagine what it would look like if the IDF were not trying to avoid harming babies and innocent civilians. Remember that Israel has tried throughout this terrible war to move Palestinian civilians away from Hamas' network of terror tunnels and weapons caches.

Hamas' use of Palestinian civilians as expendable human shields (placing rocket launchers in playgrounds and restricting the movement of Northern Gazans trying leave) has devastated Gaza. Hamas has destroyed countless Palestinian lives in addition to Israeli ones, compounding indescribable grief in all people of conscience.

As Rabbi Yitz Greenberg wrote:

> "In the classic chutzpah narrative, a man kills his father and mother and pleads for mercy on the grounds that he is an orphan. Hamas has done better. It sets up tens of thousands of civilians as human shields. Then, after massacring a thousand civilians, it demands a ceasefire. No one should fight back against its terrorism — since civilians will be hurt."[3]

The world seems increasingly determined to ignore Israel's determination to remain human in the face of unspeakable inhumanity. Many seem just as committed to ignoring the inhumanity of Hamas' having placed babies and innocent civilians in harm's way in the first place.

---

[3] Rabbi Yitz Greenberg, *"Civilian Casualties and the Ethics of Jewish Power"*, The Jewish Journal, November 30, 2023

The question, for so many right now, is: can we recognize evil when we see it, and act accordingly? Too many are willing to believe the worst about Israel without any critical thinking or historical awareness and are simultaneously interpreting the atrocities of Hamas as the work of Palestinian national liberation. Fighting for peace does not mean laying down and dying.

A prayer:

God, it's too much, this grief. It clouds my judgment and shrinks my compassion. My pain and my anger overwhelm my gentleness. Every waking moment and in my dreams I see images of children going to war, babies taken hostage. In my mind I cannot stop replaying terrible, wretched footage recorded by humans who have successfully negated their own humanity, wreaking atrocity and evil upon others. Suddenly I find myself unable to comprehend the world I inhabit.

Holy One, what has become of Your Image? Are your children that powerful, that some of us can even erase You from our essences? Oh, this truly is war. A necessary one. It is not only my family that is threatened. It is humanity itself that is on the line.

But God, I beg of You, that in our fight for humanity we manage to, somehow, retain our own.

To re-find our gentleness, somehow.
To reclaim Your Essence within us, somehow.
To heal, somehow, someday.

Amen.

A few bursts of light:

On November 14, 2023, more than 290,000 Jews and allies marched in Washington, DC in support of Israel. *One out of every 50 Jews in the world were there.* It was the biggest Jewish gathering in American history. (250k+ more joined online.) Raw, deep emotions in each of us. On the one hand, אין מילים – *there are no words.* On the other hand, the ancient history of Jewish life can truly be understood as a purposeful response to the world as it is, with a vigilant eye toward bringing it one inch close to how it should be.

On November 28, Kibbutz Be'eri began planting wheat again and the communal dining hall reopened.

Some of the hostages have been released. Jews all around the world are fighting to bring them home now.

In Israel, many babies born during these last weeks have been named Be'eri: *my wellspring.*

A thought:

The State of Israel was born as a political vision in response to global Antisemitism, chants of genocide against the Jews, expulsion and pogrom, even and especially in the halls of power and higher education. We have learned the price of naivete. We lost so very much.

But a word of caution against losing even more. As Rachel Sharansky Danziger wrote,

> "[T]here is more to winning than 'not losing', and there is more to victory than beating an enemy in the battlefield. To win, to truly win, we will have to rise from our grief and pain and rebuild and grow stronger and better."[4]

Indeed, as Tal Becker wrote in a beautiful essay:

> "Zionism was never only a response to crisis – it was a values project from its inception. In fact, many current Israeli policies

---

[4] Rachel Sharansky Danziger, "*This is why we will win*", The Times of Israel, November 9, 2023

and the debates around them can be understood on moral grounds, even if they are more often couched today in survivalist terms."[5]

Our ancestors didn't only dream of having not-murdered descendants. They dreamt of redemption, understood best as a tomorrow that learned the painful lessons from yesterday well enough to achieve something better for their own descendants. They dreamt of Jewish babies who would grow into thriving adults who would do something constructive in the world. They dreamt of peace, knowing that the world doesn't grant peace, especially for Jews; it must be pursued with strength and commitment, resilience and might, moral thinking and military knowledge. They dreamt of Jewish self-determination, as fraught as it would be.

Though true healing is a long way off, I take comfort from the advice of the ancient sage Rabbi Yochanan, who survived the attempted destruction of the Jewish People in his own day and had the courage and creativity to start again. His words?

> "Rabbi Yochanan said: From where is it derived that there the Jewish People's fate is not dictated by the stars (fate)? As it is stated: "Thus said the Lord: Learn not the way of the nations, and *be not dismayed at the signs of heaven;* for the nations are dismayed at them" (Jeremiah 10:2). The nations may be dismayed by them, *but not the Jewish people."*[6]

Though true healing is a long way off, I take comfort from the advice of an ancient sage who defied fate to build a strong, vibrant future for the Jewish People. I pray we are courageous and wise enough to do the same in our day, that our ancestors will look back with pride and appreciation for the unity we work to maintain in the face of terrible hardship for the Global Jewish community in 2023.

A closing intention:

---

[5] Tal Becker, *"Beyond Survival: Aspirational Zionism"* (2011)
[6] Talmud, Shabbat 156b

Tonight is the Fifth Night of Channukah, one candle for each Book of the Torah. And oh, how necessary Torah is tonight, more than ever. From the Genesis of our family to the Exodus from our People's pain, from nurturing Sacred Community to navigating the dangers of a wild world, to telling our story over and over to our children's children. And then starting again. And again. And again. Until we are truly free. And even then, we will continue telling our story from a place of regained wholeness for the sake of an unfinished world.

We light these lights. That is who we have always been, who we are, who we will fight to be. This is what we are called to do: *bring light.*

Am Yisrael Chai!

29 Kislev, 5784
Fifth Night of Channukah
December 11, 2023

Introduction to Israel Poems

On a bus from Jerusalem to Tel Aviv years ago, I gazed at the amazingly green landscape on either side, alive thanks to the same Zionist intention that laid the pavement upon which we were driving. Burnt tanks preserved on the highway shoulder bore testimony to the battles the Jewish People has been forced to and continue to fight to preserve our right to live as a free people in our native land, now known as the State of Israel.

The beauty of the natural landscape and the brutal reminders of the very real cost of freedom have been in my eyes.

Something changed on October 7, 2023. I think.

At a recent Shabbat dinner, I remarked on this to a longtime friend who responded with compassion:

"Menachem, nothing has changed. This is how it's always been."

And I wonder. That bus ride and its multivalenced view, perhaps different from the scars in Israel's southern communities only in how recently the wounds were suffered, suggests that my friend was right. The battles of 1948, 1967, and 1973 were but three of countless international attacks on Israel and those who call it home. Both intifadas (1987-1993 and 2000-2005) were constant murderous assaults on Israeli civilians.

Was October 7 anything new? Comparisons to the Shoah have become common, and they are not without merit. Holocaust Survivors danced and cried and sang and marched with Nova Survivors at Auschwitz this past Yom YaShoah veHaGevurah. Time has always been fluid in Jewish experience. As Elie Wiesel put it:

"A Jew lives in more than one place, in more than one era, on more than one level. To be Jewish is to be possessed of a historical consciousness that transcends individual consciousness."

It is too soon to look back at what happened. It is still happening.

Perhaps, given the continuity of scars on our soul and our soil and the way Jewish time-consciousness connects all moments, it will never not be present. Our hearts and this place, this beautiful, sacred, holy, complicated place we call home is pervaded by this kind of demanding intensity.

I remember sitting on that Hebrew bus on a Hebrew highway with a Hebrew ticket stub in my pocket and Hebrew thoughts in my Hebrew heart. I wouldn't have it any other way.

Israel is where I count myself, bitten and blessed, burnt and inspired, crackling, fierce, and alive.

May these words I could not hold back be worthy.

May our family be whole again, soon and in our days.

Am Yisrael Chai – the People Israel is Alive!

Menachem Creditor

8 Iyar 5784
May 16, 2024

TORAH REFLECTIONS

Tzav: Sacrifice

Parashat Tzav, the second Torah portion in the book of Leviticus, introduces us once again to the ancient systems of sacrifice, a topic that may seem distant and complex to some, graphic and gory to others. What inner message might we access, beyond the surface textual layer?

Rabbi Jonathan Sacks, may his memory be a blessing, highlighted the rise and fall of civilizations in a comment he offered on Tzav. He particularly noted the tragic turn of the Mayans, who resorted to human sacrifice in times of turmoil, forsaking reasoned solutions for mystical beliefs. When the world became too heavy to bear, they placed their future on the altar.

Contrastingly, the Jewish journey has seen a different trajectory. Following the destruction of the Second Temple in 70 CE, our forebears, led by the wisdom of early rabbis like Yochanan ben Zakkai, embarked on a transformative path. Unable to continue offering traditional sacrifices, we adapted, engaging in profound discussions and finding new avenues to connect with the Divine.

Today, we witness sacrifices of a different nature. Our brave children, the young women and men in the Israel Defense Forces lay their lives on the line to safeguard our people. They epitomize sacrifice, all-too-often paying the ultimate price. Sacrifice takes various forms, encompassing learning, prayer, advocacy, defense, and yes, even wielding weapons when necessary. Where our ancestors offered animal sacrifices, today we fulfill our covenantal obligations and secure our collective destiny by giving of the self in immeasurable ways.

We do not sacrifice the future when burdened by harsh reality. We instead offer up of our selves, transcending the current moment's adversity through timely commitment, to ensure a future for our children and theirs.

We Jews are a resilient people, shaped by history and undeterred by the trials of the present. Let us approach our responsibilities wholeheartedly, infused with love, guided by the knowledge that our mindful sacrifices propel us and our descendants towards a brighter tomorrow.

Kedoshim: Intense Lessons from the Nova Exhibition: Learning to Dance Again

From the rich tapestry of Torah to the depths of the human experience, from the ever-present energy in the air to the constant buzz of news cycles, life can be a dizzying mosaic of interconnectedness. And yet, even amidst this intense web, there are moments that demand pause and reflection, that stop us in our tracks and pierce us with sudden and undeniable intensity.

I share here a recent experience that left a mark on my soul. It was a visit with 80 staff members of UJA-Federation of New York, where I am blessed to serve as scholar-in-residence, to an exhibit currently in downtown New York City featuring artifacts from the October 7th attack at the Nova festival in Israel. The magnitude of the curator's design and the poignant display of human resilience amidst tragedy stirred something deep within me. In the presence of burnt-out cars and remnants of a once-vibrant festival, I was confronted with the fragility of life and the enduring spirit of hope.

In the midst of this solemn reflection, I had the privilege of speaking with Yarin Ilovich, the DJ who was playing at the festival right when the Hamas attack began. His gorgeous spirit, his spiritual commitment to art as a vehicle for healing, his focus on bringing light even and especially after such darkness, left an indelible impression on me. It was a testament to the resilience of the human spirit, a reminder that even in the darkest of times, there exists a flicker of light waiting to be kindled, that dancing again is possible, that joy and love can and do endure.

We also heard testimony from Moran Stella Yanai of her experiences of being kidnapped by Hamas on October 7, 2023 and taken hostage. She was released after 54 days of brutality in captivity. Her commitment to sharing her story was heroic and terrifying, literally stunning. She commanded us with the power of her sheer life-force, by her presence, to be witness. "Intense" does not begin to name what she has been through, nor does it adequately describe her unwavering commitment to do everything in her power to bring back those hostages still in captivity.

As we navigate these tumultuous times, I'm reminded of the Torah's injunction in this week's Parasha, Kedoshim, to "be holy (*Kadosh*), for I the Lord your God am Holy (*Kadosh*). (Lev. 19:2)" In this seemingly abstract directive (what does "holy" actually mean?) lies a profound truth, as understood through the prism of rabbinic interpretation:

holiness is not an abstract concept but a call to action, a summons to embody the Divine in everyday life. Through acts of kindness, compassion, and solidarity, we become vessels for the sacred, conduits for healing and transformation.

In the wake of tragedy, we are called upon to bear witness, to honor the memories of those we've lost, and to ensure that their stories live on. This sacred promise binds us together as a community and reminds us that our individual lifetimes are truly only fragments of the interwoven lifeline of our community, our family, our People. All people deserve nothing less than freedom and life, a call in our very bones that is both ancient and increasingly modern.

In a Shabbos talk decades ago I'll never forget, I heard the great Rabbi Yitz Greenberg define "kadosh" as "intense" — a reminder that life, with all its dense complexities and intense challenges, is a profound gift to be cherished and embraced. We are called to embrace each moment with equally intense fervor and purpose, knowing that in our collective energy lies the promise of more light tomorrow.

As we support the survivors of October 7th, we serve as witness and voice for those who were murdered while dancing in celebration of life itself. We amplify the calls of the survivors for the release of the hostages. Let us also reaffirm our commitment to building a world where love triumphs over hate, where light overcomes darkness. That lofty dream, that dream of a universal love has felt woefully out of reach (and perhaps hopelessly naive), I learned from Yaniv's intensely beautiful soul. He demonstrated what it is to still envision a world beyond the brutality and evil that occurred on October 7, to still imagine and work to actualize light and healing, to build a better world.
We must both bear testimony *and* double down on hope, on light, on healing. We must be witnesses *and* agents of change, living reminders of the cataclysmic tragedy of October 7 *and* catalysts for transformation, as we work together towards a future that learns from the horrors of the past and works to surpass today's pain with something more worthy and just.

May we be strong enough to make this story heard.

May we be intensely loving people.

May we be brave and beautiful enough to dance again.

Amen.

Bechukotai: Cosmic Ripples

The Torah portion Bechukotai, the final one in the book of Leviticus, speaks deeply to the human condition. It contains a series of blessings and curses that are not merely punitive measures but rather consequences of our actions. What we do creates ripples throughout the cosmos, impacting everything around us in ways that are often beyond our immediate comprehension. This concept, deeply rooted in Kabbalistic thought, is essential for understanding the Torah's message in Bechukotai.

The portion underlines a fundamental truth: our actions have consequences, both beautiful and severe. This is not only a lesson for us as individuals but also as a community in our covenantal relationship with God. This relationship, which began with Abraham and Sarah, carries with it the weight of our collective actions. The Torah assumes, and rightly so, that we will not always make the right choices. Yet, it is within this framework of assumed imperfection that the true essence of faith and relationship with the Divine is revealed.

Judaism does not require a dogmatic agreement about the nature of God. What it emphasizes, instead, is the importance of our actions in manifesting our faith. "Faith" in Judaism is not a matter of belief but of practice, a "leap of action" as Rabbi Abraham Joshua Heschel phrased it. It is about showing up in the world in ways that align with the values we profess. As the Torah portion illustrates, if we do right, blessings follow; if we stray, we face the consequences. But within this system of cause and effect, there is also an enduring promise of God's presence and love.

The text in Bechukotai, particularly Leviticus 26:44, encapsulates this beautifully:

> "Yet even then, when they are in the land of their enemies, I will not reject them or spurn them so as to destroy them, annulling my covenant with them: for I am the LORD their God."

This verse assures us that even in our failings, God's commitment to us remains steadfast. It is a reminder of the resilience and flexibility of the covenantal relationship we share with the Divine.

Rabbi Heschel and others have elaborated on this by teaching that true love and concern for God and for each other mean recognizing and responding to each other's needs. This idea of "transitive concern" extends to our relationship with God: if we truly love God, then what concerns God should concern us. This is a profound way of understanding what it means to be created in the image of God, bearing a fraction of divine responsibility and power.

In practical terms, this means our relationships with others should reflect this divine concern. We are called to be present for each other, to forgive, and to build bridges where possible. This is especially challenging in times of personal and communal pain, but it is precisely in these moments that the Torah's teachings are most vital. The Torah does not ask us to accept harm passively but encourages us to stand up for ourselves while also seeking ways to reconcile and build connections.

As we navigate through these difficult times, let us strive to channel the Torah's call for compassionate action and steadfast faith. Let us remember that every person carries within them a spark of the divine and that our actions towards one another ripple through the cosmos, impacting the world in profound ways. Let us bless ourselves, our communities, and our world with a renewed commitment to humanity, understanding, and peace.

Bechukotai: Becoming Faithful Ancestors

Parashat Bechukotai invites us to reflect on the deeply intertwined relationships we have with our ancestors, the Divine, and the Torah itself. As we conclude the Book of Leviticus (VaYikra), we might find ourselves relieved to move past the detailed laws of sacrifices and priestly duties. However, to dismiss this book as merely a legalistic manual is to overlook its profound and urgent messages about morality and communal life.

Renowned scholar, Professor Jacob Milgrom, of blessed memory, often emphasized that Leviticus is not just a book of law but a book of love. The intricate details within are not meant to burden us but to illustrate the care required in our relationship with God and each other. These ancient texts teach us how to build a beloved community, one that embodies the Golden Rule found in Leviticus 19: "Love your neighbor as yourself."

Leviticus calls us to recognize the visceral connection we have with the Divine. In ancient times, offering a sacrifice involved a physical connection—we placed our hands on the offering, feeling its heartbeat, experiencing a profound moment of vulnerability. While we no longer perform such rituals, the underlying principle remains relevant: our connection to God and each other must be tangible and heartfelt. When we care for another person, we are, in essence, holding onto an image of God.

Within this week's portion, we encounter the powerful notion of divine remembrance in times of failure. Leviticus 26:42 reassures us that God will remember the covenant made with our ancestors—Jacob, Isaac, and Abraham—even when we fall short. The order of this remembrance is significant. Typically, we recite the patriarchs in chronological order: Abraham, Isaac, and Jacob. However, this verse reverses the order, beginning with Jacob. An ancient Midrash, the Sifra, suggests that this sequence reflects a hierarchy of merit, starting with the most recent ancestor and reaching back if needed. This indicates that in moments of deep vulnerability, we are never alone; our ancestors' merit and God's enduring promise are always there to support us.

Rabbi Jonathan Sacks, of blessed memory, poignantly wrote about this enduring hope in the face of suffering. He reminded us that despite Israel's trials, hope will never be abandoned. Exile and persecution may occur, but hope remains. The placement of God's promise to remember us at the end of a series of curses underscores a vital biblical truth that pain does not get the last word.

We are part of a timeless chain of tradition. Our ancestors reach forward through the ages to hold us, to comfort us, and to promise us that we will never be alone. By connecting to the Torah and its teachings, we traverse time, feeling the embrace of those who came before us. This lineage of support and love is a source of immense strength and hope.

As we celebrate milestones, both the uplifting ones and the terribly tragic, we are reminded of the sacred continuity and resilience of our people. We are living links in this chain, charged with the responsibility to uphold and transmit these values to future generations, just as our ancestors did for us. If we do our part authentically, our actions today will become the legacy that our descendants look back on with pride and gratitude.

In moments of solitude or doubt, we can draw strength from this rich heritage. Our ancestors, from the founders of our faith to those who rebuilt it in times of crisis, inspire us to persevere and to contribute to the ongoing story of our people. This enduring connection is a testament to the beauty of our tradition and the faithfulness of God's promise.

Let us close with the wisdom of Rabbi Sacks, who taught us that despite suffering, we will never perish. He reminds us that the assurance at the culmination of curses in Bechukotai is one of the most hopeful biblical assertions:

> "No fate is so bleak as to murder hope itself. No defeat is final, no exile endless, no tragedy the last word of the story."

Let us reaffirm our commitment to being the ancestors our descendants deserve, so that our children's children's children will always feel the loving embrace of their heritage.

May we find strength in these eternal connections, joy in our tradition, and hope in the promises that bind us together across time.

Bamidbar: A Journey of Love and Resilience

This week, we delve into a new book of the Torah, the Book of Bamidbar, also known in English as the Book of Numbers. I am reminded of the profound distinction between its Hebrew name and its English counterpart. In Hebrew, "Bamidbar" translates to "in the desert" or "in the wilderness," which evokes a different imagery than "Numbers." The English name stems from the census described at the book's beginning, but for now, let us explore the deeper meaning of the desert, the wilderness, and what it signifies in our tradition.

The desert can be a place of vast emptiness, where the wind howls and the sand dunes stretch endlessly. Yet, it is also a place of profound majesty, a space for reflection and spiritual growth. My experiences hiking and meditating in the desert have shown me its serene beauty and the introspection it can inspire. However, it is important to recognize the challenges faced by those who live in the desert, such as the Bedouin communities who maintain their ancient ways of life.

Our ancestors' journey through the desert was marked by both hardship and profound moments of divine connection. The Torah and the Prophets offer varied perspectives on this time. One poignant memory comes from the Prophet Jeremiah, whose words we sing on Rosh Hashanah and Yom Kippur, recalling the early love between God and Israel, likened to a honeymoon in an uncharted land (Jer. 2:2). Conversely, the Book of Psalms reflects on the Israelites' rebellion and God's frustration during the forty years of wandering (Ps. 95:10).

So, is the desert a place of wandering and rebellion, or of discovery and love? The answer is, of course, both. The desert is a place of uncharted territory, where each step redefines the journey. Just as the wind erases footprints, our path is continually reshaped by our experiences and reflections.

This brings us to a contemporary moment of significance. Yesterday, 100,000 people marched up Fifth Avenue for Israel Day, a testament to our resilience and unity. I had the honor of being on the UJA-Federation NY float, welcoming leaders and dignitaries, including Eden Golan, Israel's remarkable representative at the Eurovision song competition this year. Her performance of "Hurricane" at Eurovision, amidst immense adversity, symbolized our collective strength and determination. Her performance back in Israel after the competition of the song in its original form, "October Rain," (as it was before

Eurovision censors deemed the pain of October 7 "too political") was beyond riveting – it was profoundly holy, shaking hearts and the foundation of Heaven itself. Eden's soul embodies the spirit of Am Israel, beautiful, poetic, and noble. As she sang in Europe, in Israel, and in New York City, her voice is a powerful beacon of Jewish pride and resilience, a moment etched in our history.

Reflecting on yesterday's power, I am reminded that our journey, much like our ancestors in the desert, is filled with challenges and opportunities for profound love. The desert can indeed be a place of hardship, but it can also be a space of incredible beauty and joy, depending on how we choose to navigate it.

As we march forward, we carry the strength of our collective experiences. Today is day 241 since the beginning of our most recent struggles. Let us demand of Heaven and our leaders that today be the day we bring our family home. We must remain steadfast, demanding protection for our children and families, never slowing down or growing quiet.

Today, I moderated an interfaith panel at UJA with Muslim and Jewish families whose family members were brutalized and taken hostage by Hamas on October 7. It served as an overwhelming and poignant reminder of shared humanity. Let us double down in our efforts, fueled by the unity and strength we experienced yesterday and today.

May our journey through this desert be marked by love, resilience, and the unyielding pursuit of peace. Let us cultivate this love, so that when we look back, we remember not just the hardship, but the profound connections we forged and the steps we took towards a brighter future.

May our families be whole soon.

Counting the Uncountable: Reflections on Bemidbar

The Book of Bamidbar, known in English as the Book of Numbers, sets the stage for the rest of our journey as a people. It channels everywhere that we've been and ensures we recount our time in the desert—two generations, countless lifetimes, and an infinite number of lessons to be learned. It begins with a crucial task: counting people. Jewish tradition hesitates to count individuals directly, a theme I will discuss in tonight's Israel Matters event. Yet, this morning, I want to delve into the significance of this census and its implications for our identity and resilience.

The census in Bamidbar is a complicated one. It serves the pragmatic purpose of defense; we need to know our numbers to gauge the strength of our defending forces. This act of counting shapes our understanding of what it means to walk through the world, especially when the world resembles a wilderness—a wasteland, as T.S. Eliot might say. In such indeterminate times, knowing who is with us becomes vital.

Consider the verses in chapter one of Bamidbar, where Moses and Aaron take a census of those indicated by name. The Hebrew word used, "va-yikach," suggests a profound act of indication—one that pierces through to the essence of each individual. This notion of being pierced, from the root word "nekuv," signifies how deeply we are affected by being counted, recognized, and named.

Every morning, as I put on my necklace, I am reminded of the blessings and responsibilities that come with being counted. Yesterday, I spent time with survivors from the south, moderating a panel for family members of Muslim and Jewish hostages held by Hamas since October 7th. The news that five believed hostages had already been killed was devastating, piercing our collective heart once more.

Moses and Aaron took these warriors, pierced by their names. Are we, in our modern lives, saying the names of our beloveds? Are we acknowledging the pain and hope carried in each name—whether it be Yitzhak, Omar, or Muhammad? Citizens from twenty-three countries and four faiths are bound in this shared struggle. To honor them, we must align with the work of peace and demand their safe return. "Bring them home now, Amen." Repeat this prayer with me, with closed eyes and a heartfelt plea: "Please, bring them home now, Amen."

A true warrior for good does not seek the triumph of one tribe over another but strives for a world where we are pierced by the names of all who suffer, recognizing our shared fragility. Tonight, representatives from Kibbutz B will share their stories, and former Israeli Prime Minister Naftali Bennett will join us. My beloved and our children will sing, but what matters most is our community's unity and strength in calling for the return of the hostages.

I have much to say, but the essential message is clear: bring them home now, Amen. This prayer, shared with family members of hostages, resonates deeply. One Israeli man, a veteran of many wars, shared with me how he once thought diaspora Judaism was unnecessary. At a parade with 100,000 marchers, he realized he was not alone—he had us. Our task is to ensure no member of our family feels isolated. If only our love and support could reach our beloveds in captivity, perhaps we can send our emotional strength to them now.

Let us send our hearts together. Repeat with me: "Bring them home now, Amen." For those joining in person tonight, I look forward to celebrating with you. To those online, know that this community is real, and you are an integral part of it. Thank you for ensuring none of us feels alone, for taking care of each other, and for embodying the spirit of our people.

On this 1066th broadcast, on day 242 since October 7th, with our beloveds in our hearts, let us send our hearts and prayers together.

Bring them home now, Amen.

Pierced by Names (Bamidbar)

The Book of Bamidbar sets the stage for the rest of our journey as a people. It channels everywhere that we've been and ensures that we tell the story of our time in the desert. This story spans two generations but encompasses countless lifetimes and an infinite number of lessons to be learned.

It begins with a profoundly important act: counting people. The census is a complicated one, intended for the purpose of defense. We need to know our numbers to determine the size of our defending forces. This necessity speaks volumes about our existence in this world, especially when the world resembles a wilderness, a wasteland, as T.S. Eliot phrased it. In such indeterminate times, then and now, knowing who stands with us is crucial.

Reading these verses from the first chapter of Bamidbar, we see Moses and Aaron taking a census of those who were to fight, designating one name at a time. The Hebrew word "nikvu/designated" in the verse (Num. 1:17) is significant. While it can mean "to indicate," it also carries a deeper connotation of being pierced, derived from "nkv," which means to create a hole (to 'appoint'). This imagery of piercing is powerful. When we are counted, we are marked deeply.

Every morning, I put on a necklace that reads in Hebrew, "Our hearts are captive in Gaza." As I prepare to fasten it around my neck, I mark the number of days it's been since October 7 (today is day 245) and recite a blessing: "Bring them home now, Amen." I recall as many names as I can, feeling them pierce me every time.

This past week, I spent time with numerous survivors from communities in Southern Israel that have suffered terrible attacks and losses. I spoke with families of Jewish and Muslim hostages held captive by Hamas since October 7th. The news we received three days ago that five people we thought were hostages had already been killed was devastating, penetrating our hearts with pain again.

Moses and Aaron took these warriors, who were pierced by their names. Are we saying the names of our beloveds? Are we calling out for Agam, Hersh, Muhammad, and Keith? Omer, Ariev, and Noa? Citizens of 23 countries and at least four faiths are being held in terrible conditions by terrorists who have shown – and broadcast – their inhumanity through ruthless sexual assault, mass murder, and psychological torture. In the face of this, let us all say their names and share this prayer: "Bring them home now, Amen."

Yesterday, an Israeli whose cousin is being held hostage shared something profound with me. He said he grew up thinking he didn't need Diaspora Jews, believing the diaspora itself wouldn't last, a belief held by others I've known. But when he saw 100,000 marchers supporting Israel and the hostages at this past Sunday's "Israel Day on Fifth," he cried, realizing he was not alone.

Friends, our work is to ensure that no member of our people, no member of our family, feels alone. If only we could send our emotional support, love, and fierce embrace tunneling through the ground to where our beloveds are held. Maybe we can. Maybe right now, we need to let their names pierce us, let them in.

Perhaps this kind of piercing can also serve as a way of securing them in our very being, and that through this kind of effort, we can grip more fiercely our end of the invisible thread that connects our souls.

Please God, when we recite our beloveds' names, may our prayerful intention follow the trail piercingly anchored in their hearts and ours. May they know that we love them and that they are not alone. May they be restored to our loving embraces, whole and safe.

Bring Them Home Now. *Amen.*

Courage and Pride (Shlach)

Today marks a momentous occasion. Fifty-five years ago today, the Stonewall riots ignited the LGBTQ+ liberation movement in the United States, reverberating around the world. This day, once known as Remembrance Day, now stands as a symbol of pride and resilience. At the Stonewall Inn in Greenwich Village, the police raided a bar, inadvertently sparking a revolutionary response.

An incredible transformation has taken place in just 55 years. As Jews, we understand the duality of time; it can feel like both an instant and an eternity. The progress we've made in recognizing the equal dignity and beauty of our LGBTQ+ brothers and sisters, parents and children, neighbors and fellow human beings is nothing less than astounding. The leaders of this movement, the pioneers, chose to transform a day of violence and pain into a movement of pride. They wanted the world to remember not just the struggle, but the triumph of love and humanity.

This week's Torah portion, Shlach, resonates deeply with this theme. The spies who ventured into the land of Israel were not there to inform God, who already knew the land, but to prepare the people for the challenges ahead—militarily, emotionally, and spiritually. However, ten of the spies allowed fear to cloud their vision, spreading doubt and uncertainty among the people.

In contrast, Caleb and Joshua stood firm, calming the community and inspiring them with courage. He declared, "We shall rise... we shall overcome (Num. 13:30)," a phrase that resonates with the essence of both ancient and modern struggles for liberation. This declaration is not just a statement of hope but a call to action.

As we commemorate the 55th anniversary of Stonewall and celebrate Pride Month, we must remember the courage it takes to stand up against fear and oppression. The leaders of the LGBTQ+ movement, much like Caleb and Joshua, believed in a hopeful and inclusive future. They acted with courage, expanding circles of love and human dignity, channeling the teaching of Rabbi Abraham Joshua Heschel: that our faith calls us to take a leap of action, not just belief.

Stonewall, often described as a riot or rebellion, has become a source of pride, a transformative message that transcends categories and calls us to recognize the inherent dignity in every human being, each and every one a sparkling image of the Divine.

Caleb's courage, his steadfast belief in the possibilities of the future, is a powerful reminder for us today. It teaches us that in the face of fear and uncertainty, we must rise and act. We must ensure that no one walks alone, that every person feels supported and loved. This is the essence of Pride and the sacred imperative to be courageous.

We are called to channel this spirit ourselves, to stand firm in our belief in our capacity to build a better future. Let us cultivate so much love that it transforms the world, moving it closer to the way it always should have been.

With all the love in our hearts, let us send this love where it is needed— to our families, neighbors, and especially to children who deserve affirmation for being who they are. Let us tell them, today and always, how loved they are. Let us send our hearts to those still in darkness, giving them courage and reminding them that they are not alone.

Together, we rise. Together, we build a world of love, acceptance, and dignity.

Korach's Rebellion: The Illusion of Holiness

Korach, a cousin of Moses and Aaron, is dissatisfied with his power and desires more. This week's Torah portion delves into Korach's rebellion and the language he employs in what can only be described as a political campaign. Though ancient Israel wasn't a democracy, the support of the people held real significance, and Korach's challenge to leadership is indeed compelling.

Let us focus on one particular claim Korach makes. Korach's argument boils down to questioning the special status of Moses and Aaron: "What makes you so special? We're all holy. (Num. 16:3)" This echoes a central theme from Leviticus, "You shall be holy, for I, the Lord, am holy. (Lev. 19:2)" Yet, Korach's statement shifts the emphasis. Instead of the aspirational "you *shall be* holy," he asserts "you *are* holy," transforming a command into an assumption.

The distinction is profound. The command in Leviticus calls for striving towards holiness, whereas Korach's assumption suggests complacency. This resonates with contemporary global political rhetoric, where historical and biblical references can be manipulated to sway public opinion.

Korach's offense was in asserting that the Jewish people ('Israelites' in the Torah's context) had already achieved their pinnacle of holiness. This mistake mirrors a broader misconception in any society: believing that we've arrived at (or had, at some point, realized) our ultimate potential. But the ongoing work of building a better world, striving for justice, and cultivating holiness is never complete.

America, often described as an exceptional nation, faces a similar challenge. Are we inherently special, or are we called to continually improve and expand our values? The answer lies in the latter. The values that define us must evolve, guiding us towards greater inclusion and equality. We must grow.

Korach's fatal error is his willful ignorance of this noble truth: the journey towards holiness, justice, and a better world is ongoing. We must never become complacent, believing we have already achieved our goals. Instead, we must embrace the continuous effort to improve ourselves and our communities, to grow.

Holiness is not an inherent state but an aspiration, a vision requiring constant recalibration. Korach missed this point, but we must not. Our tradition and history urge us to keep striving, not because we desire conflict, but because the work of perfecting the world is far from over.

Not for the Sake of Heaven (Korach)

Parashat Korach, a poignant ancient exploration of conflict and leadership, remains frighteningly current. Korach challenges the authority of his cousins, Moses and Aaron, accusing them of elevating themselves above the community they serve. The biblical narrative communicates the palpable tension of contrasting intentions behind this dispute and the qualities that distinguish servant leaders from those whose primary motivations are attention and power.

Korach is a populist whose language is defined by what Michael Milburn and Sheree Conrad term 'the politics of anger, (Raised to Rage, 2016).' He confronts Moses and Aaron, not with constructive criticism nor a strategic vision for the community's betterment, but rather with a clear desire to agitate and disrupt. His challenge, cloaked in the language of equality and justice, is fundamentally self-serving. Korach's question, "Why do you raise yourselves above God's congregation?" (Num. 16:3), seems on the surface to advocate for communal equity, but it is a facade for his underlying ambition. After all, Moses repeatedly refused God's call at the burning bush (Ex. 3:13, 4:1-13), and Aaron was only thereafter called by God to serve as Moses' spokesperson (Ex. 4:14-16). Not only did the brothers not chase power, they attempted to escape it entirely.

In a fanciful midrash, Korach's attempt to denigrate Moses and Aaron's authority is expanded to include an additional facet: antinomianism, the rejection of law itself.

> "And Korah took (Num. 16:1)" - What is written right before this? 'Let them place a cord of techelet (blue) to their tzitzit. (Num. 15)' Korah jumped on this and said to Moses, 'Is a tallit that is made entirely of techelet exempt from the mitzvah of tzitzit?' Moses responded, 'It requires tzitzit.' Korach responded, 'An all-techelet tallit is insufficient but four attached threads of blue suffice?!' [Korach then asked,] 'Is a house full of Torah scrolls exempt from the mitzvah of mezuzah?' Moses responded, 'It requires a mezuzah.' Korah said to him, 'A house that holds all 275 sections of the Torah is insufficient, but one section in the doorway is sufficient?!'

Korach said to Moses, 'These matters, you were not commanded about them by God. From your own mind you added them.' This is why the Torah writes, "And Korach took." This kind of language is always about divisions. (Bemidbar Rabbah 18:3)"

By framing tradition in this way, Korach sought to divide community. He wasn't truly asking meaningful questions, not in the biblical example of Moses' and Aaron's authority, and not in the midrashic cases of tzitzit and mezuzah. He was attempting to tear traditional structures down, all the while garbing his intentions with shallow claims of pursuing justice.

In our text, Korach taps into intense societal anxiety and 'gaslights' the community, misdirecting them for the purpose of the very self-elevation with which he distorts Moses' and Aaron's leadership, recasting the beauty of mindful practice as a perversion of sanctity. Arguments motivated by ego are inherently destructive. Such disputes, driven by a need for recognition, at best undermine communal cohesion and stifling growth, at worst fracture societal bonds. Korach's argument is not for the sake of heaven; it is a power play, a bid to usurp Moses and Aaron's positions without regard for the well-being of the community. This is a stark contrast to arguments that are *l'shem shamayim* (for the sake of heaven), characterized by a genuine desire to improve community, to be of service to others.

In contrast, consider the Talmudic model of the debates between Hillel and Shammai. Though often passionate, the disputes of their competing schools of Jewish tradition were rooted in a shared commitment to discover divine truth and enhance communal life. Their arguments were constructive, aiming to clarify and deepen understanding rather than to dominate or embarrass. This approach to disagreement fosters growth and development, benefiting the entire community.

When faced with Korach's rebellion, Moses does not respond with immediate condemnation nor defense of his own record. Instead, he falls on his face (Num. 16:4) in an act of humility and distress. Moses' leadership is marked by his willingness to bear the burden of the people and his constant intercession on their behalf - even when they turn against him.

True leaders are those who see themselves as servants. They lead not for personal glory but out of a sense of duty. Such leaders prioritize the needs of the community over their own prominence.

These leaders model a divine quality the mystics call tzimtzum, the way they envision God having contracted God's Infinite Light to create space for the world, a cosmic act of self-limitation. This notion of Divine Humility is a powerful counter-model to the human tendency towards ego, all too often the case in today's complicated worlds of religion and politics where individuals all too often conflate their own ambitions with the sacred obligations of powerful communal positions. Tzimtzum is the decentralization of one's own authority, empowering and encouraging growth and development in others. This model contrasts sharply with those who seek to dominate and control and shows that true leadership lies in humility and the empowerment of others. As the ancient sages of Pirkei Avot taught:

> "Every dispute that is for the sake of Heaven, will in the end endure; But one that is not for the sake of Heaven, will not endure. Which is the controversy that is for the sake of Heaven? Such was the controversy of Hillel and Shammai. And which is the controversy that is not for the sake of Heaven? Such was the controversy of Korach and all his council. (m Avot 5:17)"

Arguments for the sake of heaven, like those of Hillel and Shammai, foster understanding. Leaders who see themselves as servants, following the humble model of Moses and the Divine example of tzimtzum, create spaces where others can thrive and where true communal growth can occur.

In the end, Korach's rebellion and its tragic outcome serve as a cautionary tale. They warn against the dangers of ego-driven disputes and self-serving authority figures. They remind us that true leadership requires humility, self-sacrifice, and a commitment to the greater good. And they call us to strive for arguments and to seek out leaders who consider service the highest value and the best use of power.

Chukat: Leadership, Legacy, and the Power of Self-Reflection

Parashat Chukat can be seen through many lenses, including as a leadership bridge from one generation to the next. Chukat includes the death of Miriam (Num. 20:1), the death of Aaron (20:28-29), and it foretells the death of Moshe (20:12). These are the three recognizable figures who have been leading the people for a generation and a half, whose service on behalf of the community and whose vision, inspired by God, was nothing short of spectacular, noble, effective, and wise. Each one of them embodied a different kind of function: Aaron the high priest, Miriam the prophet, and Moshe the law-bringer and prophet, serving God in the most intimate way, similar to a priest.

It is important is to note that, at least according to some commentators, between last week's Torah portion and this week's, 38 years have passed. Last week, Moshe's leadership and Aaron's leadership were challenged by Korach, and that rebellion was forcefully put down. But this week is a different kind of moment where the challenge to leadership is not actually a challenge; it's just the evolution of who will stand before the people on the ongoing trajectory toward that which has been promised.

From Sinai till now, there's been a very complicated and bumpy path that has been led with nobility and with passion by three siblings: Moses, Aaron, and Miriam. What a powerful thing it is to experience this parasha in a moment where this is a current cultural conversation. This isn't making a political or partisan comment; it's reflecting the Torah's guidance that transitions between generational leadership is incredibly important and considered sacred. Chukat includes the death of two and mentions the death of the third of the most important leaders we have ever had. The bridge role of any leader who has gained the wisdom of an entire generation is to make sure that leaders in the future will be able to continue that path forward.

Along with this message is its necessary complement, also within the Parsha. As is true of every generation of Israelites (and later of every generation of Jews), the culture of the people seems to be to complain about whatever they've got. We are, of course, commanded to cultivate gratitude. We wake up in the morning recognizing the grandeur, the miracle of just having another day of breathing. But it is true that we are very, very good at complaining.

A real story that happened in my world when I was first ordained as a rabbi:

> My first pulpit was a very special community in Sharon, Massachusetts. There was one gentleman in the shul who always felt that it was either too hot or too cold in the sanctuary. (Every shul has people who feel this way, sometimes both at the same time.) This gentleman would always ask the custodian to adjust the temperature. We noticed this and spoke to the custodian in advance, asking him to say he would take care of it, walk out of the sanctuary, do nothing, and then come back to check in with the gentleman. Sure enough, the next Shabbat, the gentleman felt it was too hot, called over the custodian, who said he would make it better, left the sanctuary, did nothing, and returned 20 minutes later. The gentleman responded with two words: "much better."

This story demonstrates that often, when we complain, it is an inner truth that we are actually reflecting, something about needing to be heard.

So, what is this generation of Israelites, the second desert generation, complaining about? They are ostensibly complaining about the manna, the miraculous food that God sent every day (Num. 21:5). The people say the manna is miserable, and a plague of venomous snakes is sent by God to punish those for not having gratitude (21:6). To save the people, God commands him to create a fiery serpent, a saraf (21:8). Moses creates it out of copper (21:9), a symbol we now recognize as a symbol for medicine and healing. The Torah says that whenever people who were bitten by snakes looked upon this copper snake, they would be healed.

Tradition looks at the difference between the snakes that were attacking and the snake that was doing the healing. One insight is that it is measure for measure: snakes were doing the attacking, so a snake was used for healing. Another measure for measure suggestion: The Israelites had complained about manna, which tasted like whatever you wanted it to taste like, and so they were punished with snakes, whose Edenic ancestor was cursed to have everything taste like dust (Gen. 3:14).

Another fascinating suggestion is that Moses chose copper for the healing-snake because polished copper is reflective, like a mirror. Deep healing includes self-reflection. The Israelites were looking outward and not inward. Their discontent was internal, though their complaints pointed elsewhere.

A synthesized message of these two parts of Parashat Chukat: A community cannot look only at who is standing in front; a community must also have the courage to look within to understand what they truly need.

The accumulated wisdom of two generations of leadership, as represented by Aaron, Miriam, and Moses, was the only way the Israelites made it this far through the desert. The challenge for the Israelites in Parashat Chukat (and for us in today's cultural discourse) is based on both recognizing that the leadership they had in the hardest of conditions during their a 40-year journey was nothing short of miraculous, and that self-reflection presents an entirely different kind of challenge, both experiences of traversing the unknown.

Balak: Blessings Amidst Curses

in loving solidarity with Bring Them Home Now's https://weekofgoodness.com/

In Parashat Balak, we encounter the non-Israelite prophet Balaam, hired by King Balak of Moav to curse the Israelites. Though often portrayed in Jewish interpretative texts as a charlatan, the Torah itself presents Balaam as a significant figure, capable of connecting with God through prophecy (Num. 22:9-12). The Mishnah suggests that he will not have a place in the world to come (mSan 10:2), further demonstrating his prominence in Jewish thought long after the biblical context had ended.

Balaam's story is compelling for many reasons, including the most famous: despite being hired to curse the Israelites, he ends up blessing them instead. One of his most famous proclamations is "Mah Tovu / How beautiful are your tents, O Jacob, (Num. 24:5)," a prayer traditionally recited by Jews upon entering synagogues to this day. This transformation from curse to blessing raises profound questions about intention and interpretation.

For instance, Balaam's prophecy includes a verse that can be seen as both blessing and curse: "As I see them from the mountaintops, gaze on them from the heights, this is a people that dwells apart, not reckoned among the nations" (Num. 23:9). While the surface reading might seem like a compliment, suggesting Israel's uniqueness, it also hints at isolation and alienation—a theme all too familiar in Jewish history.

Rashi interprets this verse as "a prerogative given by our ancestors," indicating that Israel's destiny for good comes with a sense of separateness. Yet, our foundational calling, starting with Abraham and Sarah, was to be a blessing for others (Gen. 12:2). We are meant to bring light to the nations, not to isolate ourselves.

Reflecting on more recent Jewish experiences of the world, including heightened global Antisemitism, Rabbi Jonathan Sacks z"l eloquently noted that when:

> "Jews fight for the right to be, whether as a nation in its historic home, or as a religious group in other societies, [we] fight not for [ourselves] alone but for human freedom as a whole."

Our experiences often reflect broader human conditions, making our resilience and hope a beacon for others.

As we hold these powerful words, let's remember that our goal – even when beset by violence we are called to forcefully defeat – is not to triumph over others but to live, love, and be a blessing in the world. We must remain steadfast in our prayers and actions, demonstrating fierce love for Am Yisrael, the Jewish People – and a commitment to peace.

Let's channel the trajectory of Balaam's words and transform any intended curses into blessings. We know who we are—a people who wear our hearts openly, who pray, who strive to love. We will fight when necessary, but our ultimate aim is to be a blessing in the world. May our prayers and actions bring our family home, and may we continue to envision and work towards a world where peace and love prevail.

Balak: Love Beyond the Tribe

Our parashah begins with Balak, the king of Moab, hiring the non-Israelite prophet Bilaam to curse the Jewish people. Balak recognizes that Israel cannot be defeated through military means if God is on their side. So, he seeks to disrupt God's protection by employing Bilaam's powerful prophetic abilities.

Bilaam is a figure of great interest in our tradition. The Torah and the rabbis acknowledge his potent prophetic capacity, noting that he knows the precise moment when God is angry with Israel, making them vulnerable. But, despite this power, Bilaam testifies that he can only say what God puts in his mouth, unable to curse or bless anyone without God's consent. The words he eventually utters are poetic blessings, not curses, demonstrating God's ultimate control.

This story prompts us to consider the nature of prophetic love. True prophetic love, which channels God's own love, includes everyone. Bilaam's failure lies in his inability to expand his love beyond his own tribe. A midrash in Bamidbar Rabbah (BR 20) explains that God eventually removed the Holy Spirit from Bilaam for lacking compassion for a tribe that was not his own. Prophecy, this midrash argues, can be found within the Jewish people because we strive to extend our love beyond our tribe.

Our actions must continue to reflect this expansive kind of love.

Bilaam, in contrast, is portrayed by interpretive Jewish tradition as a mercenary prophet, using his power for personal gain and failing to see the holiness in Israel. This misuse of divine gifts ultimately leads to his downfall. We must not follow his example. Instead, we must remember to love beyond our tribe, even (and perhaps especially) in times of pain and fear.

A friend recently asked if this love should extend to those who are blatantly evil. My response: It's important to distinguish between defending ourselves from those who seek to harm us and showing compassion to vulnerable others. Bilaam represents someone who would use their power to destroy others, losing his prophetic capacity as a result. We must ensure we do not conflate categories of defense and dehumanization.

We must defend our home when threatened, but we take no joy in conflict. We aim to bring love and light into the world, extending our care to all. This is the core of Torah and the purpose of our prophetic mission. By learning from Bilaam's mistakes, we can strive to bring love and blessings to the entire world.

May we be blessed to make additional effort this week to extend kindness beyond our tribe and to be blessings to others.

Balak: Eyes Wide Open

In Parashat Balak, we find a prophet named Balaam, who is hired by King Balak to curse the Israelites. Balak realizes he cannot defeat the Israelites militarily, acknowledging their strength lies not just in physical might but in their spiritual resilience. He aims to weaken them by targeting their spirits, their hearts, and their connection to God.

At first, Balaam, who indeed has access to God, speaks to God the night Balak's messengers invite him to curse the Israelites. God tells Balaam, "No, you may not go. (Num. 22:12)" Balaam relays this to the messengers, who return to Balak. Persistent, they come back with more wealth and flattery, convincing Balaam to ask God again. This time, God permits Balaam to go but commands that he only speak the words God places in his mouth (Num. 22:20), underscoring the prophet's duty to use his divine connection for good.

As Balaam sets out, an angel with an outstretched sword appears, though Balaam cannot see it initially. His donkey, however, does see the angel and reacts, causing Balaam to strike the donkey multiple times—an act of unnecessary cruelty. Eventually, the donkey speaks, opening Balaam's eyes to the angel's presence. Confronted by the angel, Balaam confesses, *"I erred because I did not know you were standing in the way. If you still disapprove, I will turn back now."* The angel reiterates God's command: Balaam must only speak the words given by God. (Num. 21-35)

This interaction reveals a critical point: Balaam's sin was not just his actions but his lack of awareness. Ignorance is not a valid excuse, especially for a prophet. Just as a child cannot strike a parent and claim ignorance of its prohibition, a prophet must be aware of divine signals. Balaam's failure to see the angel was itself the sin (Iturei Torah).

This lesson is particularly poignant in our world, saturated with information and distractions. We cannot afford to ignore the pressing issues around us. The Torah in this narrative teaches us the importance of being vigilant and responsive.

We live in a time where social media bombards us with constant updates, making it easy to become desensitized or overwhelmed in an already complicated world. Yet, we are called to keep our eyes open, to stay informed, and to act. Ignorance is not an excuse; inaction in the face of need is a failure.

Balaam's story warns against the dangers of turning a blind eye. Initially, God said not to go. The second time, God allowed Balaam to go but only to speak divine words. Balaam should have understood that he was not to go at all. His eventual realization—only after the donkey's intervention—highlights his earlier failure to perceive what was evident.

We must strive never to be in a position where we fail to see what is right in front of us. The Hebrew term "חָטָאתִי" (chata'ti), often translated as "I sinned," also means "I missed the mark." Missing the mark of our obligations to our families, our communities, and humanity is a grave error. We are called to be vigilant, to recognize and respond to the needs around us with love, sensitivity, and fierce commitment.

Our task is demanding, but it is our sacred duty. We must keep our eyes open, not just to the challenges but also to the beauty and blessings around us. Today, as we mark day 286 since October 7th, let us draw inspiration from the dedication of a new Torah in Jerusalem, an act of solidarity and hope.

Seeing something obligates us to act. Balaam failed to curse the Israelites because God turned the intended curse into a blessing. Our role is to prevent harm before it manifests, to protect the vulnerable, and to uphold our responsibility as guardians of our sisters and brothers.

If you feel overwhelmed by the world's demands, take a moment to rest, then rise to respond with renewed vigor. Seeing is not enough; we must act. May we be blessed with the courage to keep our eyes open, to see both the challenges and the blessings, and to respond with love and strength. Let's be vigilant and proactive, ensuring that our actions bring the world closer to the way it should be.

The donkey saw the angel first—let us not lag behind.

A Broken Peace (Pinchas)

Parshat Pinchas is one of the most challenging portions of the Torah, dealing with themes of zealotry, violence, and divine approval. Pinchas, a descendant of Aaron the High Priest, witnesses an egregious public sin and takes drastic action by killing the perpetrators with a spear. This act of violence is not only disturbing but also complex in its reception, as it seems to be praised by both God and some Jewish commentators through the generations.

The text reads:

> "Pinchas, son of Eleazar, son of Aaron the priest, turned back My wrath from the Israelites by displaying among them his zeal for Me, so that I did not wipe out the Israelite people in My passion. (Num. 25:11)"

The passage implies that without Pinchas' violent intervention, God's anger would have resulted in the annihilation of the Israelites. This raises profound questions about violence, divine will, and morality.

Rabbi Jonathan Sacks, of blessed memory, addresses such dilemmas in his book "Not in God's Name (2015)," where he explores the dangers of religiously motivated violence. While Pinchas' act is portrayed as a zeal for God, it still sits uncomfortably with us because it involves taking lives in the name of faith.

One of the most striking elements in this narrative is the apparent reward Pinchas receives. In the very next verses, God grants him and his descendants a "covenant of peace" (brit shalom). However, there's a deeper, more nuanced message embedded in every Torah scroll that demands careful attention. The word "shalom," the peace with which Pinchas and his descendants are blessed, is written with a broken vav, signifying an incomplete peace. This is unique, as any other broken letter in a Torah scroll would render it unfit for use, yet here it is intentional – required, actually.

This broken vav symbolizes the fractured nature of peace achieved through violence. Pinchas' zeal, while averting immediate disaster, leaves a lasting mark of brokenness. His act of violence, though seemingly justified, cannot bring about true, whole peace. Instead, it leaves behind a legacy of brokenness, carried by him and his descendants.

This brokenness serves as a powerful reminder of the consequences of violence. Even when, out of legitimate indignation, violence feels sanctioned, it fractures the wholeness of any kind of real peace. Rabbi Abraham Joshua Heschel once said,

> "I don't accommodate myself to the violence that goes on everywhere; I'm still surprised. That's why I'm against it, why I can hope against it. We must learn to be surprised. Not to adjust ourselves."

This resonates deeply as we reflect on Pinchas' story. We must remain shocked by violence to cultivate goodness and to strive for a peace that is whole and unbroken.

The events of October 7th, 292 days ago, shocked us all and serve as a stark reminder of the impact of violence. We must resist normalizing it in any form—whether in our language, our actions, or our policies. The broken vav of Pinchas' peace challenges us to seek a different path, to pursue peace through understanding and empathy.

As we reflect on this Torah portion, let us bless ourselves with the strength to remain thoughtful and mindful in our reactions. Let us be vigilant against the normalization of violence and strive to heal the brokenness in our world. May we take one step at a time towards a peace where everyone can breathe freely, where the broken vav is made whole, and where true shalom can be achieved.

When Faith Grows (Pinchas)

Many think that change is the opposite of tradition, but actually, the beauty of Judaism, the beauty of Torah itself, is that change is part of the sacred process. It's not a modern response to tradition that leads to change; rather, the Torah demonstrates the capacity for growth and learning, even on a theological level. Though this might sound strange, God has emotions and responds, discovers things. I know that doesn't sound like what we've been taught to think about God, but in the Torah's text God grows and respects humanity enough to partner with and even learn from us sometimes. (Of course, in the text, we are humbled and learn from God as well.)

An important case study for this claim occurs toward the end of Parashat Pinchas:

> "The daughters of Tzelophehad, of Manassite family—son of Hepher son of Gilead son of Machir son of Manasseh son of Joseph—came forward…(Num. 27:1a)"

(Notice how many times the text said "son of." The Torah doesn't waste words. These are Tzelophehad's male ancestors, but given that we're about to hear about the daughters, this detailed male lineage is significant.)

The text continues:

> "…The names of the daughters were Mahlah, Noah, Hoglah, Milcah, and Tirzah. They stood before Moses, Eleazar the priest, the chieftains, and the whole assembly, at the entrance of the Tent of Meeting, and they said, 'Our father died in the wilderness. He was not one of the faction, Korah's faction, which banded together against יהוה, but died for his own sin; and he has left no sons. Let not our father's name be lost to his clan just because he had no son! Give us a holding among our father's kinsmen!' (Num. 27:1b-4)"

This is a very important moment in the Torah. Prior to this, inheritance laws didn't include women. But the five daughters of Tzelophehad confront to Moses and say, in effect:

"This is not right. Why should our family's name be erased just because there are no sons? We are daughters. Don't women have the right to continue the legacy of a people?"

Moses' response is deeply important, and instructional to those who aspire to leadership: Moses brought their case before God (v. 5). How important to read this text carefully. A few aspects deserve extra attention:

- The challenge to the way things have been is important.
- Organizing in order to make a claim – all five of them show up together, unity in the family to make a claim.
- The women go to Moses, and Moshe Rabbeinu (Moses our teacher), does not answer the question immediately. He hears their claim and, in effect, says, "I don't know." This is a magnificent attribute of a leader – to know when you don't know.

Moses turns to God, and God responds, "The plea of Tzelophehad's daughters is just. You should give them a hereditary holding among their father's kinsmen; transfer their father's share to them. (v. 7)" Further, God instructs, "If a householder dies without leaving a son, you shall transfer his property to his daughter. (v. 8)"

Not only do the daughters of Tzelophehad organize and present their case to Moses, but Moses has the humility to say, "I don't know," and turns to God for an answer. God not only affirms their plea but also sets a new precedent based on their case. When those who pursue change utilizing a strategy that shows respect for the process, everyone benefits, even and especially future generations.

I bless us with a little bit of hope that things might change, that when we organize and press for change, we shows humility and respect for the systems that define community. There are those who believe that the system needs to be torn down, but that's not the way to make things better. Nihilist activism is not the way. What a gift it is to read in this week's Parasha the possibilities alive within God's own process and within faith itself. Nothing in this reflection has been midrash; all of it is within the biblical text.

What a blessing it is to know that things can change and that we can grow, even at our most ancient layer, the biblical text itself. How much more so as students of that text, as children of God, one and all.

So, the blessing I wish for us this Shabbat is to remember that things can change for the better, that when we work together with humble, fierce spirits, things can change for the better. Look what we can do. Look what our matriarchs showed us. Look at what's possible. We can grow.

Let's reaffirm the capacity we have as a community that has come together to learn, to comfort, to heal, to grow. How lucky we are to have Torah and each other. How happy we should feel that this is our portion.

Let us pray that one day soon, our family will be made whole, that peace might one day still be possible, and that the world could have a better day tomorrow than it did yesterday.

Shabbat Shalom.

On the Edge (Mattot/Masei)

Friends, as many of you know, I have just returned from Israel. I was there with a solidarity mission of staff from the UJA Federation of New York. Twenty of us journeyed together to meet with grantees, partners on the ground, our Israel staff, and others, to be present during a time of ongoing stress and creative response. The way we have shown up as a people in the world has been enormous, impressive, and inspiring. While we shouldn't have needed to be the miraculous and beautiful people we are, we are those people nonetheless.

Today marks 301 days since October 7th. That might be the most important thing I say because it highlights just how difficult this period has been. Yesterday in Jerusalem, I ran from place to place to capture every moment of day 300. Not because it was pleasant, nor because it was joyful, but because that's what you do.

This week, we read a double Torah portion, Mattot and Masei, which together conclude the Book of Numbers. In Mattot and Masei, we find the journey of the people nearing its end before entering the Promised Land. We know there is another entire book of the Torah, Deuteronomy, that we will begin after completing Numbers. In this week's Parasha, we basically reach the edge of the Promised Land. The next book, Deuteronomy, will retell the story, and how we tell a story matters.

At the very end of the story in our double Parasha, the Book of Numbers presents a significant moment. As we are about to cross the Jordan, the tribes of Reuben, Gad, and half of Manasseh approach Moses, saying they do not want to cross the Jordan. Let that sink in. Twelve tribes have been traveling together for forty years. Moses has been leading them through trials, tribulations, rebellion, disappointment, plague, and assault. The point of this entire journey was to reach the Promised Land, and now Moses is told he himself will not make it. The one thing he wants more than anything else is denied, and now Reuben and Gad say they won't enter the land with him.
Moses loses it. He says, "Your fellow Israelites will head off to war, and you're just going to sit here?" (Numbers 32:6). This verse is testing everyone not in Israel right now. Families in Israel are taking shelter. My daughters are in Jerusalem, my sister lives in Tel Aviv, and countless friends who are like family are under immediate threat. Leaving Israel last night felt conflicting, especially knowing I was returning to officiate a colleague's wedding.

The verse highlights something critical. It is important for all of us—Am Yisrael, the people of Israel, and those connected to our people—to internalize this. Am Yisrael includes not only Jews but also Israeli Arabs, Christians, Druze, Bedouins, and other citizens. While 80% of Israelis are Jewish, the remaining 20% are not, yet they are all part of the larger Israeli identity.

The challenge of Moses in our days is nothing less than this: when Reuben and Gad say they will not cross over, Moses asks if they will fight. They respond that they will. This question was gently asked of me yesterday during a podcast recording with Amanda Borschel-Dan, the deputy editor of The Times of Israel. She asked what "chizuk" (strengthening) means to me. I explained that when I order coffee in Israel, the barista can pronounce my name. This small detail symbolizes belonging, not living in translation, a feeling not always present in America.

This feeling ties into a broader conversation: the relationship between Jews and their sense of identity. The phrase "Jewish American" versus "American Jew" has long been debated. Given the fragility of the American Jewish community and historical complexities, the totality of who we are must be recognized. Outsiders often see all Jews as the same, here and there, embodying the narrative of anti-Zionism and antisemitism.

Zionism is an articulation of Jewish dignity, the belief that Jews have a rightful place on Earth. This belief does not ignore our imperfections but calls us to grow. The response of Reuben and Gad to Moses must be ours too. They eventually agree to fight alongside their brothers. This unity is critical.

Standing with Israelis in Jerusalem, witnessing the resilience and life amid stress, is a reminder of our collective strength. It has been a difficult 301 days for Jews worldwide, yet the work we do brings our people closer, helps them feel strong, loved, and supported.

We are not victims. We are miraculous, heroic, and alive. As we stand on the edge of our metaphorical Jordan River, we must remember what it means to be home. Each visit to Israel, despite its challenges, reaffirms this connection. We do not sit by when our family is in need.
I ask you to embrace the pride of being part of Am Yisrael. Say it: "I am a Jew, and I am so proud." This pride is not about triumphalism but about recognizing our place in the world and our responsibility to our family and community. As we move forward, may we continue to grow,

never satisfied with where we are, and never sit by when our family needs us.

We are Am Yisrael, and we are proud. On this Erev Shabbat, on our 301st day since October 7th, may our family come home. May we remember to sing, to be proud, and to hold each other close.

Devarim: The Call to be Strong and Kind

Devarim, Moses' long goodbye to his People, demonstrates Moses' recognition that the story of Am Yisrael must continue beyond him, beyond his lifetime. This is a profound recognition that no one - not even Moshe Rabbeinu - lives forever.

Moses conducts his final speech with urgency, knowing he is the last witness, the final survivor of his generation. In this portion, Moses recounts how B'nei Yisrael (the Israelites) were treated by other nations. For example, he remembers Moav being good to them and instructs us to show kindness in return, while he recounts that Bashan was unkind, so we should not be kind in return. (Deut. 2 & 3)

This framing is crucial. Jewish history is replete with instances of being mistreated by other nations—Baghdad, Babylonia, Spain, England, the USSR, and even, at times, the United States. Recently, we've seen a reckoning and awareness of these mistreatments, especially after October 7th. It's a reminder that history isn't always linear; sometimes, it's circular.

We have a duty to assert Jewish values like justice, which are core to our identity. We cannot be good Jews if we don't act ethically. At the same time, we must maintain the dignity and integrity of our Jewish community. There's a renewed urgency to hold on to our history and remain vigilant as a People.

Moses's message in Devarim is to be kind at every opportunity but also to recognize and remember our history. Justice is just as important now as it ever was. And we must balance that sacred universalism with tribal vigilance. When someone shows kindness, we should be grateful, but we should also be mindful and cautious with those who have been hostile.

As we reflect on this portion and Moses's words, let us remember to be both strong and kind.

Tears of Heaven, Strength on Earth: Our Call to Act (Va'Etchanan)

It is fitting that in this week's Torah portion, Va'etchanan, we find Moshe Rabbeinu, our greatest teacher, in prayer. Moshe, who stood so close to God, begs for entry into the Promised Land, only to hear a definitive, heart-wrenching "No." This is a profoundly human moment for Moses, one of the greatest figures in our tradition, facing the reality of unanswered prayers. Sometimes, the answer is simply no. That reality is painful and heavy, but it's also sacred.

The story of Moshe in Va'etchanan is more than just about a denied request—it's about how we respond when life tells us no. Moshe doesn't crumble; he doesn't stop leading. He channels his grief into ensuring the future. He sets up his successor, Joshua, to guide the people forward. In his own heartbreak, he finds the strength to continue building.

My wife, Neshama, shared with me a powerful insight about this Torah portion—she imagines God's "No" to Moshe coming through tears. God's love for Moshe is immense, and though God's decision is firm, it doesn't come without sorrow. This reading suggests a different kind of relationship with the Divine, one where God feels deeply alongside us. God cries with us in our struggle, not as a distant force, but as a loving presence.

We, too, are tasked with building amidst our grief. Just as Moses planned for the future of the Israelites, so we plan for the safety of our families, our communities, our world. And as we fight for the return of our hostages, for the security of our students on campuses, for the dignity of our People, Am Yisrael, we must also remember to link arms across time and space—with Moshe Rabbeinu, with each other, and with those who will come after us.

Friends, we know that we are not guaranteed forever, and so we must act with urgency, with purpose, and in pursuit of justice. Just as Moses ensured the continuity of his community, so must we. We are builders of this world, creators of a legacy that will outlive us. And even when our prayers go unanswered, we can choose to be the answer to someone else's prayers.

Let's not quiet our voices in the face of injustice. Let's not lose our resolve when we are told "No." Instead, let us respond with action, with empathy, with an unwavering commitment. Let us teach our children how to carry forward this work. Let us build a world where no one lives in fear under their own roof, where every family can sit in peace under their fig tree, where none shall make them afraid.

We are builders.

We are strong.

And we will not be silent.

Not tomorrow. Not later. Now. (Ekev)

Parashat Ekev invites us to reflect on the power of listening and the consequences of our actions. In this final stretch of Moshe's journey, he stands at the threshold of the Promised Land, unable to cross. His life's work has been leading us here, yet he must face the reality that his time is limited. How heartbreaking it must have been for him, pleading with God to change the rules, only to hear, "Enough. It's time for something new."

But there's a profound lesson in this. Moshe's story reminds us of the urgency of now. Our time is not infinite, and that very limitation is what makes each moment sacred. The German Jewish philosopher Franz Rosenzweig wrote that while science attempts to reduce the fear of death, religion teaches us the urgency that comes with mortality (*The Star of Redemption*). Every moment we have is a precious opportunity to act, to love, and to make a difference. We don't have forever. That's what makes right now so vital.

In Parashat Ekev, we read, "And it will be, if you listen." This conditional promise hinges on an *if*—not a certainty. It's a reminder that our actions, or inactions, have real consequences. If we listen, if we act, if we embrace the urgency of the present moment, we can bring about change. But it's not guaranteed. It's an invitation, not a certainty.

Just as Moshe was aware of the limits of his life, we, too, must recognize that our time to act is not infinite. As we reflect on Moshe's journey and our own, let us remember: We may not be able to change everything, but we can change something. The time to act is now. We must not wait for a better moment. Not tomorrow. Not later. Now.

May we seize this moment with the fullness of our hearts and souls. We don't have forever, but we do have *now*. Let this be the moment we choose love, action, and healing.

Let this be the moment we bring them home.

Now.

The Peril of Prosperity (Eikev)

*in memory of Avraham Munder, Alex Dancyg, Yagev Buchshtav,
Chaim Peri, Yoram Metzger and Nadav Popplewell z"l*

Six souls. Six human beings. Six men who were ripped from their
families on October 7, now returned to us in a way none of us wanted.
As we sit with the news of these recovered hostages from Gaza, we feel
the weight of their absence and the unbearable reality their families now
face. They are not just names; they are our fathers, brothers, husbands,
and friends. I invite you to take a moment to look at their faces, to see
their eyes, to honor who they were. This moment is impossibly hard. We
are 319 days into this nightmare—not just 319 days of war, but 319 days
since these men were violently taken from us. What we count are not the
days of conflict, but the days since our loved ones were stolen. The war
is about bringing them home, and while this isn't how we wanted them
returned, we honor them now. Their families, at the very least, can now
mourn with certainty, can care for them as they deserve. May their
memories be for a blessing. May they now rest in peace. Home.

Parashat Eikev reminds us of the consequences of our actions—"when
you listen," it says, "things will go well for you in the land." Yet, we
know life doesn't always follow this Divine calculus. Good people
suffer, and that's a conversation for another time. But today, let's stay
with the parsha's promise.

"When you have eaten your fill and are satisfied, bless God for the good
land that God has given you (Deut. 8:10)." But the Torah warns us to be
careful, lest we forget God amidst our prosperity. We might say in our
hearts, "My own power, the might of my hand, has won this wealth for
me. (Deut. 8:17)" But no, there is something greater than ourselves at
play in our lives.

We don't choose the circumstances of our birth, the parents we are
given, or the love that finds us. We are placed here, in this moment, and
we are called to recognize that life is larger than the self. We are called
to be humble, to understand that while we must work hard and use our
gifts, we are not the sole architects of our success.

Humility matters. It should be a criterion for those we look to for
guidance, be they leaders or loved ones. Yes, we need to wield power
with willingness, but we must do so with a humble heart, knowing that
we do not do this alone.

As I reflect on these words, I am reminded of President Biden's recent speech. Regardless of politics, his admission—"America, I gave you my best"—is a powerful example of humility. Like Moses, he affirmed that the mission extends beyond his time in office. We, too, must acknowledge that the work continues beyond us.

So, as we move forward, let us reflect on the gifts we've been given and the responsibilities they entail. Let us commit to doing good today—one kind act in memory of those we've lost and another in celebration of life's blessings.

Let us send our hearts to the east, with a pure thought: bring them home. Now.

The Greatest Thing in the World is to Do Something Good for Someone Else (Ekev)

Parashat Eikev includes the ancient promise: "If you listen, then things will go well for you." At first glance, it seems simple—do good, and good will follow. But as we know, life is rarely that straightforward. If only the world worked like that, but it doesn't. As we age, we come to understand ever more deeply that bad things do happen to good people. It is instructive to note that Rabbi Harold Kushner, in his seminal work "When Bad Things Happen to Good People," wasn't asking *why*—he was acknowledging the reality that unfairness *is* part of our lived experience.

The Torah speaks of rewards for following mitzvot, but even the ancient rabbis teach us that these rewards aren't necessarily found in this world. Instead, the true reward for fulfilling a mitzvah is the mitzvah itself—the opportunity to do more good (Pirkei Avot 4:2). We're not meant to follow the mitzvot for the sake of reward, but because it is right.

I was reminded of this during a recent visit to Israel, where I had the privilege of meeting children supported by an organization called SAHI that instills this very value. They've faced immense challenges, yet they are taught, in the tradition of the great Polish Jewish educator Janusz Korczak (1878-1942) and Rabbi Rabbi Kalonymus Kalmish Shapiro (1889-1943), whose lives intertwined in the Warsaw Ghetto, that the greatest thing in the world is to do something good for another person. And they live it—every day, in ways both big and small.

This lesson is timeless. Doing good isn't about what we get in return, but about being part of something greater than ourselves. It's about embodying a love so true that it expects nothing in return. When we act with kindness, when we choose to show up for others, we bring a piece of the world to come into the here and now.

May we be blessed, in this way, with the strength to show up for others, to be the person who doesn't wait for rewards but acts because it's the right thing to do. May you be a good ancestor, a good neighbor, and may the kindness you offer ripple out in ways you can't even imagine. As Rabbi Harold Kushner said, "If there were any 'help others' sections in bookstores, there would be no need for self-help sections." Let's build a world where we show up for each other, where we remember that doing good is the greatest thing we can do. And in that, may we find true blessing.

A Sacred Triad: Listening, Honoring, and Doing (Eikev)

Parashat Eikev begins with a reminder that resonates deeply, especially now. Last night, many of us witnessed Rachel Goldberg and Jonathan Polin speak at the Democratic National Convention. Their words, as they continue to advocate for their son Hersh and all the Hostages, were laden with the weight of grief, love, and determination. Rachel, struggling to compose herself at the outset, embodied the profound pain of a parent whose heart has been torn for 321 days since October 7. The collective cry of tens of thousands at the DNC —"Bring them home now"—echoed their desperation, a cry that must continue until it is answered.

In the first verse of Eikev, we read,

> "And it shall come to pass, if you listen to these rules and protect them and do them... (Deut. 7:12)."

The first step is "Lishmo'a" – to listen. invites us into a process that Moshe Rabbeinu urges us to undertake: to truly listen. This act of listening is not passive; it is the first step in a sacred triad that leads to positive action. Consider this in your own relationships. When someone close to you speaks—whether in love, anger, or desperation—listening is the first and most crucial step. It's about more than just hearing words; it's about receiving the deeper message, the unspoken needs that lie beneath. This is what Moshe asks of us: to listen with our hearts, to be present for the pain and the plea.

The second step is "Lishmor"—to guard or protect. But what are we guarding? Not just the command itself, but the relationship from which it arises. Every meaningful relationship carries with it unspoken demands—those that require us to listen carefully and guard the trust that has been placed in us. Whether with a parent, a spouse, a child, or a neighbor, these obligations shape our actions and define our integrity.

Finally, there is "La'asot"—to do. We can feel deeply, we can speak passionately, but until we act, our intentions remain incomplete. As President Obama once said in response to a loud audience reaction, "Don't boo—vote." This call to action underscores the difference between feeling something and doing something about it. The tears we shed upon hearing the stories of October 7 survivors and the families of hostages are only the beginning. The real question is: What will we do next?

The universe has been calling out for goodness, kindness, and justice long before these 321 days. The Torah calls us to love our neighbors as ourselves, to honor truth, and to live with integrity. These calls are not exclusive—they coexist within the same universe, and there is more than enough love and kindness to go around.

So, what is the specific message we need to hear right now? For each of us, it might be different. Judaism does not prescribe a singular response, but it demands a response nonetheless. The steps are clear: listen, honor the relationship, and do something about it.

As we reflect on the grief and pain of these 321 days, let us remember that this grief must not paralyze us. Instead, it should propel us into action. We cannot afford to remain stagnant in our sorrow. Our tradition demands that we move forward with purpose.

Let us take a moment, before we sing, to truly listen—to hear what is being asked of us in this moment. Consider the relationship within which this call arises. And then, before we join our voices in prayer, decide what action you will take in response.

We are all necessary. What you heard is important. And once you have heard it, you are obligated to act. So, pray with me that they come home—and let's do something about it too.

The Call to Choose Blessing in a Broken World (Re'eh)

I want to begin with what I just witnessed, and I hope you will be brave and open-hearted enough to look, to listen, and to let it in. There are still 107 hostages in Gaza, held by Hamas. Many of them are no longer alive. Yesterday, the families of these hostages traveled to the border of Gaza, calling out with loudspeakers to their loved ones. Because of my feeling of personal connection with Rachel and Jonathan, Hersh Goldberg-Polin's parents, this morning's experience has scarred me forever.

Hearing them call out Hersh's name broke something in me, once again.

In the ancient world, there was a practice called *yelala*, a wailing for the dead. Paid mourners would go to funerals to evoke the tears of the bereaved, to break through the composed and collected facades people often maintained in public. When I heard Rachel scream Hersh's name, something in me broke again. This wasn't a paid wailing—it was a cry from the deepest part of a mother's soul. Rachel cried out, "It's Mama," praying her son would hear her voice again. Please, God, let him hear those words again soon. By soon, I mean now—because it's already too late, and yet, now.

I had planned to share some well-crafted thoughts this morning, but they've been scattered by the cries of those parents. Yet, there is something in this week's parashah, Re'eh, that is crucial for us to hear. Re'eh begins with the words, "See, I place before you today a blessing and a curse. Choose the blessing, choose life. (Deut. 11:26)" As a people, as a tradition, we have always fought for life. Look at how desperately we fight for it now, even when the world criticizes us for doing what we must—what any nation would do under these circumstances. Today is not the day to discuss our imperfections, though we must always remain self-reflective, holding ourselves and our homeland accountable to be the best we can be, even as we wield power we wish we didn't need.

Moses, at the end of his life, speaks to us about a future we are still striving to realize. He tells us there will be a day when we won't all do what is right in our own eyes, but instead, we will have a coherent society, a shared understanding of what is right. This vision of unity is not just a dream; it is a necessity. Yet, the challenge of Re'eh is not only in the future—it is also in the present. "I place before you *today* a blessing and a curse." How do we continue to choose blessing when our hearts are shattered? How do we choose life when parents are shrieking for their children still held in bondage?

We must respond to the chaos of the world not with more chaos but with love, structure, and the ethical use of power. We are called to choose blessing, to act with courage and coherence, to remember that even in our pain, we can be channels of blessing. The cries of Rachel and Jonathan at the Gaza border, the way they blessed Hersh in the midst of their agony, are a testament to the power of blessing. They raised their hands and recited the words we say every Shabbat, words they continue sending Hersh ever morning of the last 328 since he was stolen from their arms: "May God bless you and protect you. (Num. 6:24)"

This is our calling: to be blessers, to choose blessing even when it feels impossible. To stand with those in darkness and pray, act, and hope for their return. May God bless and protect them. May we be blessed to be a source of blessing. And may those still in darkness be brought home right now.

May we have the courage to choose blessing, to choose life, and to hold onto our humanity, even when the world around us seems to break apart.

Warriors of Heart (Ki Teitzei)

This is not a simple time for the Jewish people. It hasn't been for a long while—certainly not for the last 339 days since October 7th. I find myself returning to other milestone moments: 1967, 1948, 70 CE, 586 BCE. Time, for us as Jews, is anything but simple. Each date carries more than just history—it carries heartache, resilience, and transformation.

And yet, what we have accomplished together as a community, as a family, as a People, is nothing short of remarkable. We have risen above these moments, not just surviving but thriving. These moments are not simply checkpoints in history; they are sacred pauses—demanding, real, but ultimately formative.

As we near the one-year mark since October 7th, with its 339 consecutive days of both war and longing, of pain but also growth, I see the strength of our People. I see families moving to the south of Israel, committed to (re)building a future. I see American Jewish leaders showing up again and again to lead, teach, and heal. The connection between Israel and American Jewry has never been stronger. Even as our young people face difficult moments on campuses and beyond, they are rediscovering a deeper connection to their Jewish identity. This resurgence is our people's traditional response to threat: in the face of adversity, our Jewishness blooms.

But let's not overlook the beauty in this rebirth. Our Jewish souls are strong, not just in reaction to hardship, but because we are eternally rooted in this world. Just as the mystical Zohar emerged in response to Spain's expulsion, and political Zionism was born from the horrors of European pogroms and global persecution, Jews rise. We are not just a People of survival—we are a People of life, always moving forward, always creating.

So as we face the coming year, let us decide to face it together, as a strong and unified community. New Torah is being written, babies are being born, and eternal hope pulses within the Jewish heart, no matter what. Even in the depths of mourning, as Rachel and Jonathan rise from shiva, we rise with them. And for the families still fighting for their loved ones held in Gaza, we fight with them, holding each other with strength, security, and love.

We are bigger than the pain we face. We always have been, and we always will be.

In this week's parashah, we hear words that resonate deeply in today's reality: "When you go out to war against your enemy..." (Deuteronomy 21:10). The Torah acknowledges the inevitability of war but also calls us to hold ourselves to a high ethical standard, even in the harshest moments. What sets us apart from our enemies is our unwavering commitment to moral accountability. When we fail, when we act beyond our rights, we hold ourselves accountable.

Power, as the Torah suggests, is complicated. It would be theological malpractice to deny the power we wish we never needed. But we do need it, friends. We've been a powerless people in the past, and we know too well what that looks like. The real question is not whether we should have power, but how we wield it.

We are the inheritors of millennia of wisdom. What will we do with it? There are times when we must fight, but let us remember who we are while we do. We are called by our ancestors and descendants alike to be warriors—not just any warriors, but warriors of heart, warriors of ethics, warriors who carry the dignity of our people the whole way through.

May we continue moving forward through time, proud of who we are, who we have always been, knowing that we are bigger than any of the challenges we face. We always have been, and we always will be.

Am Yisrael Chai!

Guardrails of Care (Ki Teitzei)

In Parshat Ki Teitzei, the Torah offers a unique blend of ideals and the practical, guiding us on how to navigate the realities of our world. This portion contains a remarkable number of mitzvot—74 commandments, a sizable portion of the Torah's total mitzvot, making it especially rich in practical guidance.

One such commandment concerns the *ma'akeh*, a parapet—a fence that must be built around the roof of a new home to prevent anyone from falling (Deut. 22:8). Even if someone accidentally falls, even if they had no permission to be on your property to begin with, their injury is your responsibility simply because you inhabit that home. The *ma'akeh* represents more than just a physical safety measure; it's a call to take responsibility for others, even when the conditions that lead to harm are not of our direct creation.

The rabbis expanded on this concept, teaching that if you inherit or purchase a home, you are still responsible for the safety of those who might fall from the roof. In essence, it doesn't matter if you built the house—you live there now, and so the responsibility is yours.

This concept applies far beyond the literal. We live in structures, societies, and systems we did not build, but we are still responsible for them. Whether it's systemic injustice or vulnerable people in our midst, we are called to care. Rabbi Sharon Brous once powerfully noted that we now inherit the United States, a home whose foundational beams (see Talmud Gittin 55a) include slavery and systemic inequality. Even if we didn't build these systems, we live here now. The responsibility is ours.

This mitzvah invites us to reflect on our personal and collective responsibilities. Even when we didn't cause the harm or build the flawed system, we are obligated to protect those who are vulnerable within it. What does this look like today? Maybe it's building safeguards in our communities, or speaking out against injustice, or ensuring that others are safe—physically, emotionally, or spiritually—even when they are strangers to us.

As Rabbi Abraham Joshua Heschel said, we are images of God, and that comes with great responsibility. And, as he famously taught, "In a free society, *some* are guilty - *all* are responsible." With awareness comes obligation. The more we know, the more we are accountable for the world around us. We are called not only to tend to our own lives but to the lives of those around us—starting with those nearest to us, and rippling outward.

So, how will we carry this responsibility? The Torah's teaching on the *ma'akeh* reminds us that our care must extend to everyone who comes near us, whether we invited them or not. May we, in the coming days, build strong parapets of care, support, and protection for all those around us. And while doing so, may we remember to tend to ourselves, for we too are among those we are called to protect.

Amalek and Egypt: A Tale of Two Hates

In Parshat Ki Teitzei, we encounter an overwhelming number of mitzvot—74 to be exact—that provide guidance for living in community and navigating the moral complexities of life. Yet, among these detailed laws, there's a deeper conversation that emerges about hate—how it can fester, how it can be recognized, and how it might be confronted.

Rabbi Jonathan Sacks of blessed memory, in his teaching on "Two Types of Hate," reflects on the complexity of love and hate, offering us a lens to understand that not all hatreds are the same. In the same way that some loves are conditional and others are unconditional (see Pirkei Avot 5:16), some forms of hate are rooted in irrational fear and others in perceived justifications, even if they are unjustifiable.

In this week's Torah portion, we are commanded not to hold eternal hatred for Egypt (Deut. 23:8), despite their enslavement of our people, but we are told to never forget or forgive the nation of Amalek for their attack on the Israelites (Deut. 25:19). Egypt's oppression, while evil, was based on a rationale—a fear of the growing power of the Israelites. Once that fear was addressed, the hatred was no longer necessary. It had always been wrong, and acknowledging a rationale should not be misunderstood as validation of the hate. But the contrast between Epyt and Amalek should be instructive, however thorny it may be.

Amalek's hatred was baseless, an assault for the sake of destruction. Amalek hated simply because we existed. This is the kind of hate that cannot be reasoned with, the kind of hate that endures.

We can apply this teaching to our current moment, especially in light of recent events in the 342 days since October 7. The hatred - antisemitism and other - we witness in the world today is not monolithic. Some hate is based on the fear of the other, on misunderstandings or misrepresentations that can, in theory, be corrected. Again, this is not validation but a diagnosis of a disease. However, there are hatreds that go deeper, rooted in the very existence of the other. This is the hate of Amalek—irrational, unyielding, and destructive.

As we process the events of our time, especially after the horrors of October 7th, we must ask ourselves: How do we recognize the difference between these kinds of hate? And more importantly, how do we confront them? We grieve for the loss of innocent lives, and we acknowledge that while there are rational fears that fuel some conflicts, there are also irrational hatreds that seem impossible to address.

The Torah commands us to respond differently to these two kinds of hatred. With Egypt, there is room for reconciliation, for healing, for a future where the past no longer dictates our relationships. But with Amalek, there is no compromise. The irrational hatred that seeks to erase us cannot be reasoned with. It must be confronted and eradicated.

This wisdom from the Torah reminds us that in our world, we face both kinds of hate. There are those with whom peace may one day be possible, and there are those whose hatred will persist, unyielding. May we have the courage to discern between the two and the strength to act accordingly, always holding onto the hope that, one day, we will move beyond the shadows of hate into a future of peace. One day.

Incomplete Histories, Unfinished Prayers: Finding God in the Ordinary (Ki Tavo)

This week's Torah portion, Ki Tavo, offers two significant prayers. The first is a familiar one, the recitation of *"Arami oved avi"*:

> "My father was a fugitive Aramean. He went down to Egypt with meager numbers and sojourned there; but there he became a great and very populous nation. The Egyptians dealt harshly with us and oppressed us; they imposed heavy labor upon us. We cried to the God of our ancestors, and God heard our plea and saw our plight, our misery, and our oppression. God freed us from Egypt by a mighty hand, by an outstretched arm and awesome power, and by signs and portents, bringing us to this place and giving us this land, a land flowing with milk and honey. Wherefore I now bring the first fruits of the soil which You have given me... (Deut. 26:5-10)"

We chant it every year at the Passover Seder, telling the origin story of our people as we arrive in the land of Israel. *Ki Tavo* literally means "when you arrive." So, at the end of Moshe's life, he reminds the people: When we arrive in the land, our first expression must be gratitude.

But if you look closely at *Arami oved avi*, there's something striking about the story it tells—and doesn't tell. It skips over Sinai, and it skips the splitting of the sea. It moves quickly from the harshness of servitude in Egypt to the brief journey through the desert and ends with the arrival in the promised land. Isn't that interesting? Why omit such central events like the giving of the Torah at Sinai and the splitting of the sea?

Here we are, finally arriving, and we are commanded to bring the first fruits of our land and recite this incomplete history. It focuses on the hardships and the arrival, but not on the peak moments. The omission of these highlights feels intentional, drawing attention to the journey, the struggle, and the gratitude upon arrival, rather than the miraculous interventions along the way.

This prayer speaks to our need to remember where we've come from— that the blessings we enjoy now were not always so. But in this moment of reflection, as we prepare for Rosh Hashanah and Yom Kippur, in the midst of war and struggle, what parts of our story do we tell? What do we include, and what do we leave out?

This has not been a year of roses. Jewish history, too, has never been just good things. Right now, our family is not yet whole. The war is not over. Nearly 100,000 of our sisters and brothers in Israel cannot return to their homes in the north. What do we say in moments like these, when we bring our offerings and tell our story?

Would we include Sinai, the moment of divine encounter and purpose? Would we include the splitting of the sea, a moment of liberation at great cost? There is wisdom in the *midrash* that God rejects triumphant singing when others die, even those who would harm us. How do we carry that forward into our prayers this season? What will be the content of our prayers? What will we be singing about?

The second prayer in Ki Tavo follows when we bring *ma'aser*, the gifts of our own bounty for the vulnerable in our community. The farmer says,

> "I have cleared out the consecrated portion from the house; and I have given it to the [family of the] Levite, the stranger, the fatherless, and the widow, just as You commanded me; I have neither transgressed nor neglected any of Your commandments: I have not eaten of it while in mourning, I have not cleared out any of it while I was impure, and I have not deposited any of it with the dead. I have obeyed my God; I have done just as You commanded me. Look down from Your holy abode, from heaven, and bless Your people Israel and the soil You have given us, a land flowing with milk and honey, as You swore to our fathers. (Deut. 26:13-15)"

My dear teacher, Rabbi Bradley Shavit Artson, reminds us that both prayers follow mundane activities—bringing first fruits and providing for the poor. These actions, on the surface, don't seem transcendent. But in reciting a blessing, we are drawn beyond the limits of the moment, connecting the everyday to the Divine. Rabbi Artson points here to Rabbi Max Kadushin's notion of "normal mysticism"—Judaism's invitation to experience the presence of God in the ordinary acts of daily life.

As we navigate the complexity of our world—especially now, as we think of those in Israel, those still held hostage, those who can't return to their homes—I invite us to open our hearts. Judaism teaches us to see beyond the immediate, to hope for peace when it seems unlikely, to demand dignity when it feels so far away. To be a "normal mystic" means to notice the miracles in the mundane, to believe that through our choices and actions, we can create the beauty and goodness we seek.

As we approach this new year, let's take a breath and open our hearts to the possibility that we can be the miracle we are waiting for. Our openness to this belief is what will carry us forward.

May we all strive to be normal mystics in our extraordinary world.

Moses' Final Teaching: Owning Our Own Future (Nitzavim)

As we come to the close of the Book of Deuteronomy, the urgency of Moses' words is palpable. Moses is preparing to leave his people, and there is a heightened intensity as he speaks—more than just wisdom, it's his heart crying out. This isn't truly new information; much of Deuteronomy is a recap of the journey that began with Moses' birth. But there is a weight to these words, compounded by the fact that they are some of his last.

We read this parsha, and it feels heavy—not because of new teachings, but because of the raw emotion. Jewish tradition itself is filled with this kind of emotion. I often find myself wondering, in any spiritual space that doesn't touch my heart, where is the disconnect? Is it me? Is it the presentation? Is it the historical moment we are in? Spirit is not something we are meant to engage with intellectually alone—it must stir something deep within. Especially in moments like our current one, Jewish spiritual gatherings are meant first and foremost for tribal connection and shared emotion.

For Moses, it meant everything. For forty years, he labored to free a people, not just from external bondage but from their own internal limitations. Remember, when Moses first returned to Egypt to declare liberation, his fellow Israelites couldn't hear him. Their spirits were crushed, their breath shortened—literal and emotional constriction from generations of oppression and loss of dignity.

Now, at the end of his life, when Moses speaks, it's not just knowledge we are receiving—it's thunder. His voice echoes through the ages. And, as we approach the beginning of the High Holiday season in the next week and a half, there is a profound emotional resonance. The melodies return, familiar and stirring, touching our very raw souls with their power, as do the deep emotions we've been carrying through a very difficult year for Am Yisrael, for the Jewish People. These truly are our Days of Awe – only moreso.

But it is in this week's parsha that we find something critical for us to hold onto—not just our humanity, but the accessibility of God and spirit. In Deuteronomy 30:11, we read:

> "Surely, this instruction which I enjoin upon you this day is not too baffling for you, nor is it beyond reach. It is not in the heavens that

you should say, 'Who among us can go up to the heavens and get it for us and impart it to us that we may observe it?' Neither is it beyond the sea that you should say, 'Who among us can cross to the other side of the sea and get it for us and impart it to us, that we may observe it?' No, the thing is very close to you—in your mouth and in your heart—to observe it. (Deut. 30:11-14)"

Moses is saying to us: *Torah is yours*. Torah, "the unfolding narrative of the Jewish People" (as per Rabbi Ellie Spitz), is not in the heavens; it's not across the sea. It's right here, in our mouths, in our hearts. It is within us to utilize for strength and healing.

The Torah's greatest gift to the Jewish People is a trajectory of self-sufficiency. We don't need a miracle worker to split the sea, we don't need someone to climb up into the clouds. We have what we need. Moses' leadership was never about creating dependence—it was about empowering us to move forward on our own, being the miracle we need in the world.

Every generation's mandate is to make itself unnecessary for the next. We pass on wisdom, strength, and love, but the goal is not to be essential forever. Our children will grow up knowing things we wish they didn't. And when they take the reins, they will look back at us and wonder: why did we wait? Why did we act as if we were waiting for someone to come down from heaven to tell us what to do, when the answers were already within us?

May our children not forget what we sometimes do. May they teach us, while we still hold power, how to do the right thing. In Moses' time, there were two generations: those who left Egypt, but carried an enslaved mentality and couldn't handle the freedom they were given, and those born in the wilderness—hardened, rugged, and ready to forge a new future. We stand at a similar crossroads today, and are fighting with everything we've got for a future worthy of our children's trust.

The Torah says that the covenant is not just with us, but with those to come. As we begin this new year with intentional hope and redoubled Jewish passion, let us be humble enough to remember that the work we do is not about us—it's for the next generation.

Our task is to rebuild, to plant seeds once again, and to draw bright lines toward a Jewish future that can stand the test of time. It's not easy, but it's possible. It's not up in the heavens or across the sea. It's right here, with us, now.

May we rise to this holy work—together.

Marked by Dots, Guided by Crowns: A Torah for Now (Nitzavim/VaYelech)

The double portion of Nitzavim-VaYelech is concerned with acknowledging the balance between what we understand and what we don't. "Revealed things belong to us and our children, but the hidden things belong to God. (Deut. 29:28)" There are things beyond our comprehension, the letters above this verse in every Torah scroll marked with mysterious dots, as if to say, "Pause here. Consider."

Those dots are different from the crowns, which decorate and deepen the meaning of Torah letters (Menachot 29b). These dots are something else—they're like questions left by our scribal ancestors, marking places where the text might not make perfect sense. It's a way of perhaps saying, "I don't fully understand this, but I won't erase it. I'll leave my mark without changing the essence."

Friends, this is how we engage with our tradition. We don't tear it apart when we struggle with it. Instead, we stand in relationship with it, responding thoughtfully, critically, and carefully. The Torah is alive, and so are we. As we study, we make our marks, our dots, alongside the ancient text, but we do so in love and with reverence.

That struggle, our struggle, is real. We often ask ourselves questions in difficult times like these: "How did we get here?" "Why are things unfolding this way?" There are no easy answers. Some things are within our grasp—our responsibility—and others simply have no discernable answers. But even in the fog of uncertainty, there is a call to action. Moshe Rabbeinu reminds us: the Torah, the necessary answers for every generation's trials are not in the heavens, nor across the sea. They are here, in our mouths and hearts (Deut. 30:11-14). We are capable of navigating this world, even when it feels impenetrable.

In the urgency of these parshiot, Moshe calls out the word "Today" five times in the first six verses. He knows the stakes. He knows we're tempted to stray, to let the world's chaos pull us away from our path. But he pleads with us: Stay the course. The choices we make, the actions we take, have real consequences, both blessings and curses.

As we find ourselves in this month of Elul, preparing for the new year, we are reminded of Moshe's words: "these blessings and curses will come upon you. (Deut. 30:1)" This is the human condition—life is both bitter and sweet, full of moments that bless and moments that burden.

But, Moshe says, we will return to God, and God will open our hearts once again. "Circumcise our hearts," the text says (Deut. 30:6), but let's interpret it as "open"—open to feeling fully, to healing.

So much healing is needed right now. So let us take the ancient wisdom of Moshe, the sacred texts of our tradition, and translate them into real, tangible support. We hear you, Moshe. We hear the urgency of your message, and we will continue carry it forward.

Yes, our lives are complex. Yes, we face both blessing and curse. But we are here, alive, today, striving to be agents of healing in this world. May we have the strength to act wisely, to fight when necessary, but to always seek peace and healing. May we open our hearts fully to the world, as you taught us, Moshe.

Friends, may this year bring us clarity, strength, and compassion. May we be full-size in the world, filling every moment with purpose. Let us be the agents of healing our tradition calls us to be.

May it be so.

Fierce Love: The Response to Our Prayers
(Nitzavim/VaYelech)

As we stand on the threshold of this final Shabbat of the Jewish year, we find ourselves united in a time of profound reflection and heartache. Today, we send our hearts to everyone in danger's path, starting with our beloved hostages. They are our family, and we pray fervently that they are brought home soon. 101 people—citizens from 24 countries—some still clinging to life. We want you home. There is no comparing one danger to another, but I'm thinking of so many today: those in Florida enduring a massive storm, families in Georgia dealing with flash floods, and the people of northern Israel who still haven't returned home safely. Last night, my family in Tel Aviv, my sister's family included, was woken up by a ballistic missile fired from Yemen aimed right at the heart of Israel.

This is not a time of simple concerns, and I know many of us are carrying heavy burdens, each in our own way. I invite you to remember that wherever you are and whatever you're facing, our community is large enough, strong enough, and loving enough to hold space for you. We can't solve every pain, but we care. Deeply. Actively. As a community, we strive to do what we can, even if we can't fix everything.

In this moment, I hope that you and yours are safe. I hope you'll take care of yourselves, and I hope you'll give strength to our community as we aim to be a healing force in this fractured world. This isn't the only place where good is happening, but I have witnessed us do the unimaginable in the face of the unimaginable. We've raised hundreds of millions to distribute to those in need, come together to care for each other, and built the strength of our people, day after day, even in this incredibly challenging year.

Tomorrow night marks the beginning of the High Holidays with Selichot, where we'll gather late at night to sing, pray, and inspire each other. But it's also a moment to say goodbye—and good riddance—to a year that has tested us beyond measure. This year has been difficult, and Jewish history will mark it as one of trial. Yet, through it all, we've shown resilience. We've stood strong in New York City, Washington, D.C., and in Tel Aviv, gathering in numbers that have reflected our powerful unity and unwavering solidarity.

Alongside the hardship, we have also seen the stirring of something powerful. We've read recently in Deuteronomy, where the Torah reminds us of what leadership should be. Just a few weeks ago, we encountered the rules meant to keep leaders humble. The only person commanded to embody humility in the Torah is the king, modeled after Moses. But this is a time for not just humility—it is a time for accountability.

In this week's double Torah portion, Nitzavim-Vayelech, we witness a pivotal moment of leadership: the transition between Moses and Joshua. Rabbi Jonathan Sacks of blessed memory pointed out the difference in the blessings given to Joshua by Moses and by God. Moses tells Joshua, "Atah Tavo (Deut. 31:7)," "you will *come with* the people." God, however, says, "Atah Tavi (Deut. 31:23)," "you will *bring* the people." It's not even an entire letter that separates these two words – it's the difference between a short "yud" and a full "vav." But the nuance, as Rashi explains and Rabbi Sacks amplifies, is critical. Moses teaches that leadership is about consensus, consulting the elders, and walking with the people. God, on the other hand, tells Joshua that there are moments when you must lead by decree, even when it's difficult, even when it goes against the collective will. In times of war or crisis, leadership must be decisive. And, as we witness in countless ways, when it departs from the collective's sense of its own welfare, the group's voices must be organized and voluminous.

Friends, we stand in such a moment. We are called to lead, to move forward with clarity, to make hard decisions for the sake of our children and their children. We've seen the strength of our people in Israel, how the IDF has regained the confidence of its people, and how North American Jewry has aligned with Israel like never before. We must continue to demand strong, values-driven leadership from those in power, for our children's sakes.

As we prepare for Rosh Hashanah, may we reflect on what true leadership looks like. May we be guided by Torah's lessons and by our deepest values. May we, as a global people, find our way through this time together. And may we be written - and write ourselves! - into the Book of Life—our families, our communities, our world—each with our unique handwriting. May this coming year be one of safety, healing, and peace.

Shabbat Shalom. Let's lift our voices in prayer and song, and let us face this new year with courage and fierce love for our family.

Together, let's be the response to the prayers we shout to Heaven.

May we be blessed. May we lead with strength and compassion. And may we be part of the healing this world so desperately needs.

Essays

Letter to the Forward in response to "Whose art is it anyway? Inside the cultural battle between pro-Israel and pro-Palestinian protesters"

Though I appreciate Mira Fox considering my music part of the artistic canon ("*Whose art is it anyway? Inside the cultural battle between pro-Israel and pro-Palestinian protesters*," May 17), a clarification: others' political use of my music is not an act of interpretation. It is wrongful appropriation. This is similar to George W. Bush's use of Tom Petty's "*I Won't Back Down*" as part of his presidential campaign in 2000. The difference is that Bush's campaign was a coherent organization to whom a "cease and desist" letter could be delivered. Masked anti-Israel protestors avoid even the accountability of showing their faces. As Fox wrote, the intentions of dead artists can be hard to divine. I'm alive and making mine clear.

May 19, 2024

The Power of Tears

In the stillness of a moment, when the soul feels burdened beyond its capacity, tears come. Small, salty drops often seen merely as signs of sorrow also carry profound spiritual significance. Tears are not just a human response to grief or joy; they are the flow of divine energy itself, a primordial emanation of deep, flowing emotions, a profound expression of the collective and individual experiences of suffering, resilience, and hope.

In the Torah, we are reminded of the power of tears through the story of Hagar, who, in the wilderness, lifts her voice and weeps for her son Ishmael (Gen. 21:16). God hears the cry and responds with compassion, illustrating the sacred connection between human tears and divine response. When we cry, we are not alone; our tears are witnessed by the Divine. They become a medium through which healing and comfort can enter our lives.

The act of crying parallels the flow of divine energy described in the Kabbalistic understanding of Creation of the universe. In the beginning, God's energy flowed outward to create the world, a process that then required a contraction, a *Tzimtzum*, to make space for Creation (Sefer Etz Chaim 1:2:2). This flow and contraction, this ebb and tide of Divine Presence, is mirrored in our tears. Just as the Divine contracted to create space for the world, our tears create a space within our hearts for healing and renewal.

Various sacred texts reflect the healing properties of tears and recognizes their capacity to deepen compassion, especially in times of collective suffering and turmoil. When we witness another's tears, we are called to respond with empathy and kindness. In seeing and acknowledging their pain, we extend the flow of divine energy, fostering a community bound by love and mutual support.

May we be blessed to learn to see the sacred in our tears and the tears of others, to see the Divine in the seemingly ordinary - *to feel deeply*.

May our tears lead us to greater compassion, opening our hearts to dream again of the way the world ought to be.

And may we strive for a world where tears of sorrow are fewer, replaced by tears of joy and gratitude.

In this vision, may we find the strength to heal, to comfort, and to be comforted, knowing that in every river of tears, the Divine flows, guiding us towards wholeness and peace.

(This piece is an adaptation of Rabbi Creditor's foreword for Julie Brandon's poetry collection, *My Tears Like Rain*.)

The Place of Justice in a Post-October 7 American Jew's Heart

There was a time when all I wished for was another way to reach beyond my Jewish community to achieve justice with and for others.

It's been 304 days since I thought that way.

At first I thought it was the trauma of October 7 that led to the shift. Ten months later I'm not so sure. But the loss of a justice-seeking friend with whom I shared countless hours discussing the necessary integration of sacred ritual and universal justice triggered my heart-mind to reflect on this.

What happened? Is the change an internal one? (Have I changed?) Is it an external one? (Did the world change?) My gut says it's a lot of the former and very little of the latter.

The world has contained abundant Antisemitism, but its relatively low rate in the United States for the last two decades made it possible for me to think less tribally. (I.e., "We've made it. Now it is time to leverage Jewish privilege on behalf of other oppressed communities.") The Jewish obligation to pursue justice is not less important in light of exploding Antisemitism (I see Anti-Zionism as Antisemitism, garbed in a thin veneer of inadequate nuance). But I've come to understand that my extra-tribal focus left my family unprotected in an environment that resembles earlier, harsher times far more than I would have imagined. It is tragic that the rampant Antisemitism around the world has kept Jews like me from devoting more time to societal injustice. But who will fight for Jewish dignity if I don't?

A prayer, offered from the wounded heart of one justice-loving Jew: May the world one day soon hold itself accountable for the scourge of Antisemitism, so that we Jews will have to worry less about our own safety and dignity and find ourselves free to worry more actively about the safety and dignity of others.

in memory of Ilana Schatz z"l

Rachel is weeping for her child: In Hersh's grieving mother, we see our matriarch

Ancient words of the prophet Jeremiah haunt my soul today:

> "A cry is heard in Ramah—
> Wailing, bitter weeping—
> Rachel weeping for her children.
> She refuses to be comforted
> For her children, who are gone. (Jer. 31:15)"

This biblical verse resonates with Rachel the matriarch's timeless grief as she weeps for her children, for the pain of exile and the fear of annihilation, refusing comfort until her precious ones are back in her arms. And while her fierce tears are the tears of every parent whose child is lost to the cruelty of the world, their heightened, tragic resonance today is tribal and visceral for Jews all around the world, united in anguish as Rachel weeps once more, as our hearts are shattered yet again.

Rachel Goldberg and her husband Jonathan Polin have demonstrated the epitome of both parental love and parental pain in truly biblical proportions for their beloved son, Hersh, who was taken hostage on October 7 from the Nova Music Festival in Southern Israel. They were indefatigable and omnipresent for 330 days, speaking and shouting and crying and praying on every platform in every corner of the world, most recently inspiring chants of "Bring Them Home Now" from tens of thousands at the Democratic National Convention in Chicago just two weeks ago.

Just days ago, Rachel and Jonathan, along with many family members of hostages still trapped by Hamas, traveled to the border of Gaza to call out to their loved ones through giant speakers, crying from the deepest part of them to the deepest recesses of Hamas' labyrinth of underground tunnels. Rachel cried out, "It's Mama," praying her son would hear her voice again, sending Hersh other biblical words, the Priestly blessing of protection and peace.

But just yesterday, we learned that Hersh had been murdered by his terrorist captors at perhaps the very same moment. It is too much to bear. In the ancient world, there was a practice called *yelala*, a wailing for the dead. Paid mourners would go to funerals to evoke the tears of the bereaved, to break through the composed and collected facades people often maintained in public. When I heard Rachel scream Hersh's name, something in me broke again.

Today's parallels with ancient Jewish trauma are overwhelming too. In the face of this new and even more horrifying reality, with 97 hostages still trapped in Gaza, many of whom are already dead, even the bible falls short. The very next verse in Jeremiah reads:

> "Thus said GOD:
> Restrain your voice from weeping,
> Your eyes from shedding tears;
> For there is a reward for your efforts—declares GOD:
> They shall return from the enemy's land."

But the violation of Israel's borders and of Jewish dignity, the inhumanity of Hamas' murderous rampage, the sexual violence against women and men, the slaughtering of whole families, the stealing of grandparents and babies from their homes, and now the brutal execution of defenseless hostages all mean that any prophesized return or reward for the unceasing efforts of the Hostages and Missing Families Forum will forever be partial.

Hersh Goldberg-Polin, Eden Yerushalmi, Carmel Gat, Almog Sarusi, Alex Lubanov, and Ori Danino were discovered murdered yesterday. They will not return home alive.

So why does Hersh's death hit so hard, perhaps as intensely as the horror of October 7 itself? Because the pain has come true once again and the hope has not. Because Rachel and Jonathan did the impossible for their son and it didn't save him. They met with Popes and Presidents, heads of state around the world and youth groups traveling to Israel over the summer. They inspired countless others to daily wear a piece of masking tape tattooed with the day's horrid number since October 7.

Why do we feel this loss so very deeply? Because Jonathan and Rachel – and Hersh and Eden and Carmel and Almog and Alex and Ori are me. They're you. They're your children. Taken from our arms, from their cribs, from their kibbutzim, from their homes. Are these the only tears that have been shed? No. But they are our tears, and they have flowed with no end these last 331 days.

Echoes of Rachel's cry reverberate through the streets of Israel, and in Jewish communities spanning the globe. And our shattered hearts and hot tears will not be restrained, not by biblical command, not by empty rhetoric, not even by crowds of grieving, compassionate others. These ancient/modern tears command us to stand with Rachel, to refuse to be comforted by platitudes and empty promises, to demand justice, to work tirelessly to bring the rest of the Hostages home, and to settle for nothing less than a world where no mother has to cry out for her child.

All of this leads to heart-rending silence and soul-splitting cries. My own rambling words spilled out:

> i dreamt I was dreaming
> that a crying sky was imagined
> that rachel's cry could still be heard
> that comfort would still be possible.
>
> i woke
> to my People's shattered heart
> and photos of six precious Jewish children
> whose cries are no longer heard.
> may their souls finally be at rest.
>
> i walk through a haze
> my mind races
> my heart cries
>
> rachel, rachel, crying for her child.
> i cry with you.

As long as any Rachel weeps, our work is not done. We must continue to be her voice, her hands, her hope, building a future where the promise of return and safety is fulfilled for those still in darkness.

May the memory of Hersh, and all those lost on and since October 7, 2023, be a blessing. May their names be inscribed in the book of life, and may we be worthy of the task of bringing the rest of Rachel's children home.

Singing Ourselves Back to Life: Lullabies for the Soul

I recently found myself with a group of rabbis for a memorial, and when I asked them, "When was the last time someone sang you a lullaby?" the room fell silent, and then, tears began to flow. It reminded me in an immediate and intense way how much we need music—not just to hear it, but to let it carry us, to allow it to cradle our hearts. In a world filled with pain and uncertainty, we may turn to prayer, but we don't always take the time to sing ourselves into comfort. Music has the power to heal in ways words alone cannot. And, in this moment, words often fail.

Torah is not just about laws and stories; it's also about melody. Rabbi Ellie Spitz once defined Torah as "the unfolding narrative of our People," which means it includes the melodies that have shaped us. Music, as Professor Dov Zlotnik once taught, was at the core of how the Mishnah—the earliest code of rabbinic teaching—was transmitted from teacher to student (see his "The Iron Pillar"). The way we sing those ancient words matters. It's how we remember and how we connect. Music, like Torah, is a bridge between history and heart.

There's even scientific evidence that song can help those with memory loss recover forgotten parts of themselves. It's as if music holds the key to places we thought were lost. Maybe it's not an "as it" at all. And in a time like this, when the world feels fragmented – and the global Jewish family in particular feels so deeply broken – we need music to bring us back—to ourselves, to each other, and to our deepest truths.

Let this be an invitation to sing more, even if you already do. Sing to yourself, sing to others. Let music be a spiritual resurrection, bringing us back from the brink of despair. The second blessing of the Amidah speaks of bringing back the dead, a complex and emotional idea, especially these days. But perhaps it's also about bringing ourselves back to life—metaphorically, emotionally, spiritually. In moments of great loss and pain, we can (and must) bless each other and ourselves with music, with song, and with love.

So let's make space for music in our lives. Let's choose light amidst the darkness and let melody be among our healing guides. We are not alone. You are not alone. Let's open our hearts to harmony, knowing that each one of us truly needs this healing—now more than ever.

Birthing Worlds through Torah

כִּי־קָרוֹב אֵלֶיךָ הַדָּבָר מְאֹד בְּפִיךָ וּבִלְבָבְךָ לַעֲשֹׂתוֹ:

It is very close to you, in your mouth
and in your heart, to do it.
(Deuteronomy 30:14)

Moshe Rabbeinu, our beloved teacher, stood at the threshold of his final days and *knew* to emphasize above all the urgency of remembering that the Torah is not in some distant place. Not only is Torah within reach, but it is also an active thing, a process that can only in part be understood as Revelation from without, from above. Truly, as Moshe taught us, Torah is also very much within. In our mouths. In our hearts.

Millenia later, rabbinic interpreters would deepen this concept:

אָמַר רַב אַמֵּי: מַאי דִּכְתִיב "כִּי־נָעִים כִּי תִשְׁמְרֵם בְּבִטְנֶךָ יִכּוֹנוּ יַחְדָּו עַל שְׂפָתֶיךָ",
אֵימָתַי דִּבְרֵי תוֹרָה נְעִימִים — בִּזְמַן שֶׁתִּשְׁמְרֵם בְּבִטְנֶךָ, וְאֵימָתַי תִּשְׁמְרֵם בְּבִטְנֶךָ
— בִּזְמַן שֶׁיִּכּוֹנוּ יַחְדָּו עַל שְׂפָתֶיךָ.

Rav Ami said: What is the meaning of that which is written: *"For it is a pleasant thing if you keep them within you; let them be firmly attached together to your lips"* (Prov. 22:18)? When are words of Torah pleasant? When they are protected within you (lit, "in your belly"). And when is it that Torah is protected within you? When the words of Torah are attached to your lips.

רַבִּי זֵירָא אָמַר מֵהָכָא: "שִׂמְחָה לָאִישׁ בְּמַעֲנֵה פִיו וְדָבָר בְּעִתּוֹ מַה טּוֹב", אֵימָתַי
שִׂמְחָה לָאִישׁ — בִּזְמַן שֶׁמַּעֲנֶה בְּפִיו. לָשׁוֹן אַחֵר: אֵימָתַי שִׂמְחָה לָאִישׁ בְּמַעֲנֵה
פִיו — בִּזְמַן שֶׁדָּבָר בְּעִתּוֹ מַה טּוֹב.

Rabbi Zeira said from here: *"One has joy in the response of their mouth; and a word in due season, how good it is"* (Prov. 15:23). When does one have joy? When a response is in their mouth. Another version: When does one have joy in the answer of their mouth? When they experience the fulfillment of: A word in due season, how good it is.

רַבִּי יִצְחָק אָמַר מֵהָכָא: "כִּי קָרוֹב אֵלֶיךָ הַדָּבָר מְאֹד בְּפִיךָ וּבִלְבָבְךָ לַעֲשׂוֹתוֹ"
אֵימָתַי קָרוֹב אֵלֶיךָ — בִּזְמַן שֶׁבְּפִיךָ וּבִלְבָבְךָ לַעֲשׂוֹתוֹ.

Rabbi Yitzchak said that this idea is derived from here: "But the matter is very near to you, in your mouth and in your heart, that you may do it" (Deut. 30:14). When is it very near to you? When it is in your mouth and in your heart, that you may do it,

107

i.e., when you articulate your Torah study. (Talmud Eiruvin 54a)

We can, without too much effort, translate the combined wisdom of these three ancient sages into a three-step methodology, based on Moshe's words, for experiencing the joy of Torah:

1) internalize Torah (protect Torah within you)
2) apply Torah to new circumstances (a word in due season)
3) share Torah (do it)

The abundance of today's Torah learning communities (digital and in-person) is the very embodiment of what Rav Ami, Rabbi Zeira, and Rabbi Yitzchak had in mind: calls to mindful action based on passionate engagement with the Torah text itself and the new ideas it continues to generate. We have Torah in our bellies, it must always on our lips, and, we must cultivate our ability to share it with strength and eloquence.

Decades ago, I was setting out for a gap year in Israel, ready to explore my own Jewish identity, hopeful to find my place as a leader, curious about what lay ahead. The orientation leader in that pivotal moment, a *shaliach* named Shalom Orzach, looked us all in the eye and adjured us to "hit the ground running." I believe in those words – and in that teacher – more than ever, especially right now, as the publication of his new book of Torah commentary, *Telling Times*, will roughly coincide with the first *yahrtzeit* of the massacre October 7. If we thought we were building the world before that Dark Day, we must now redouble our pace and be part of the greatest rebuilding in Jewish history since the founding of the State of Israel itself. May our ongoing work bring our loved ones' memories blessing. We have certainly hit the ground. Now it is time to run.

We must bring forth even more of the Torah we inherited from Moshe Rabbeinu, tap into the methodology of Rav Ami, Rabbi Zeira, and Rabbi Yitzchak – to protect, interpret, and apply Torah – for the sake of our once-again wounded People. We have always been bigger than any pain meted out against us. Just look at Moshe, Miriam, and Aharon in the Israelites' post-Egyptian rebecoming. Look at Ami, Zeira, Yitzchak and Beruriah, Meir, and Akiva in the post-Destruction of the Temple era of Jewish redefinition. Examples of Jewish post-traumatic *growth* abound in our history. And here we are again, (re)creating ourselves, comforting ourselves, reminding ourselves – and the world – of who we are, where we come from, and the world we are committed to partnering with the Holy One to restore, preserve, and strengthen.

Torah is a living, breathing force that pulses through generations, not a relic but a reminder, echoing through the ages, demanding we remember that today's interpreters of Torah are tasked with the same sacred work as sages of old. Just as our ancestors shaped worlds with their insights and actions, we too are empowered to birth new worlds through the wisdom passed down to us.

Like Moshe, we stand at the crossroads of past and future, responsible for passing on not only the teachings of the Torah but the emotional intensity of its message. The Torah's power lies not only in its ancient origins but in its relevance today. Torah is indispensable to a Jewish heart.

My gratitude to my friend, my teacher, Shalom Orzach, for demonstrating throughout his life and in his new *Sefer* that we are up to the task of Telling Torah in our Times, for reminding us that the wisdom we seek is also right here, within our sacred texts, within the sacred interpretations we are so very blessed to inherit, and within our creative capacities.

The time to act, to create, and to lead is now.

Just as our ancestors did, we, too, can birth beautiful worlds. We must.

יְגִיעַ כַּפֶּיךָ כִּי תֹאכֵל אַשְׁרֶיךָ וְטוֹב לָךְ:
You shall enjoy the fruit of your labors;
you shall be happy and you shall prosper.
(Psalm 128:2)

(This piece is an adaptation of Rabbi Creditor's foreword for Shalom Orzach's book, *Telling Times*.)

HOLIDAYS

Shavuot: The Torah of Tenacious Love

Shavuot, friends, is a holiday with many different meanings, and it's important to recognize that Jewish tradition continues to gain meaning over the centuries and millennia. We don't shed these traditions; we absorb and incorporate them into the way the holiday feels today. If we were living during the time of the Torah, what would we say Shavuot is about?

It is the holiday of harvesting, as the barley harvest happens around Shavuot. Climate change might affect this over the years, but in the ancient world, Shavuot always coincided with the barley harvest. This connection is biblically rooted in the Hebrew Bible, specifically in the Book of Ruth, which we read on Shavuot. Ruth's story involves meeting her future husband, Boaz, during the barley harvest, further linking the holiday to this season.

In modern times, Shavuot has also come to symbolize the giving of the Torah at Sinai. Interestingly, the Torah itself does not specify this connection. However, over time, we have combined these meanings, seeing Shavuot as a time to harvest what we have learned and show a willingness to receive again. Just as Ruth and Boaz fell in love during this season, it is a chance for us to renew our love for the Divine, as we stand at the base of the mountain and metaphorically marry God.

Our relationship with God, like any loving, healthy relationship, evolves over time, gaining new depths and meanings. Shavuot encapsulates these various aspects: harvesting the first crops, recovering from hardships, and receiving the Torah after enslavement. We hold all these meanings simultaneously, creating a rich tapestry of tradition and personal significance.

Ruth's qualities, particularly her tenacity and loyalty, are qualities we are called to cultivate in ourselves. Ruth chose to stay with her mother-in-law Naomi, declaring, "Where you go, I will go; where you live, I will live; your God is my God." This tenacity, described by Torah scholar Aviva Zornberg as resembling a stickiness like glue, ensures that the possibilities of the future are manifest in every step she takes.

We are called to be tenacious people who channel love, to plant and harvest crops, find love again, and return to the mountain, symbolizing freedom and openness. When we gather as a community, we affirm our presence and commitment: "Here I am" (in Hebrew, "*Hineni*"). We are here, and like Ruth, we're not going anywhere. We have so much love to share, and Torah teaches us how to build on that love and demand its reciprocity. It guides us on how to channel God's love healthily, amplify good, care for ourselves, find community, and hope even in difficult times.

Shavuot is a time of receiving Torah again. If you believe in a theology of verticality, where God descends onto a mountain and we rise to meet, that is one way of experiencing revelation. However, there is also a theology of internality, where God within is always present, even if we can't always feel it. By opening ourselves up, we allow God to flow out, returning us to a state of spiritual flow.

When we are in community, we recognize the Divine in each other, similar to the Buddhist concept of "namaste": the God in me recognizes the God in you. This Shavuot, let's open ourselves to the universe and let it flow through us. This is its own form of Torah and revelation.

May this holiday find you strengthened, loving, and ready to share your gifts with the world. May we all find hope, love, and strength, and return these gifts to our communities.

On this 249th day since October 7th, on this Erev Shavuot 5784, may we be hopeful, loving, strong, and ready to share the gifts within us.

May our People continue growing in strength and healing – and love.

Pride Month: A Jewish Celebration

As we celebrate LGBTQ Pride Month, we reflect upon the tapestry of identities and expressions that make our community vibrant and whole. From a Jewish perspective, this month serves as a poignant reminder of our commitment to the principles of justice, dignity, and inclusivity embedded in our sacred texts and traditions.

Our tradition teaches us that every human being is created *B'tzelem Elohim*, in the image of God. This divine spark within each of us calls us to honor and celebrate the diversity of God's creation. LGBTQ Pride Month is a time to affirm this principle loudly and clearly, ensuring that all members of our community feel seen, valued, and loved.

Jewish history is enriched by the contributions of LGBTQ individuals who have paved the way for a more inclusive and just world. We honor the legacy of Jewish trailblazers such as Magnus Hirschfeld, the physician and sexologist who founded the Scientific-Humanitarian Committee, one of the first organizations to advocate for LGBTQ rights. We remember Harvey Milk, the first openly gay elected official in California, whose courage and advocacy continue to inspire us. And we celebrate the ongoing work of contemporary leaders like my dear friends Rabbi Denise L. Eger and Rabbi Aaron Weininger, soulful trailblazers in LGBTQ advocacy within the Jewish community and the broader world.

These individuals and many others have shown us that being true to oneself is an act of profound faith and courage. Their stories teach us that our community's strength lies in our diversity, and that our collective voice is most powerful when it includes and amplifies the voices of all its members, each a refraction of the Infinite Divine.

In the spirit of our Jewish values, we must not only include but also actively amplify LGBTQ voices in our communal and religious leadership. Our tradition calls us to pursue justice, as stated in Deuteronomy 16:20, "*Tzedek, tzedek tirdof*" (Justice, justice shall you pursue). This pursuit is not passive; it demands action, advocacy, and allyship. It requires us to create spaces where LGBTQ individuals can lead with authenticity and where their contributions are celebrated.

We must recognize that the moral urgency of this moment extends beyond mere inclusion. It is about ensuring that LGBTQ Jews have equal opportunities to shape the future of our communities. This means supporting LGBTQ individuals in their journey to become rabbis, educators, and leaders. It means creating policies and practices within our institutions that reflect our commitment to equality and justice. And it means standing in solidarity with the LGBTQ community in the face of ongoing discrimination and violence. We must each do our part to build a community where everyone can live with dignity and pride.

As we celebrate LGBTQ Pride Month, let us reaffirm our commitment to these values. Let us honor the legacy of those who have fought for equality and justice, and let us pledge to continue their work. May we be inspired by their courage, and may we strive to create a world where every individual is recognized as a reflection of the Divine, worthy of love, respect, and celebration.

In this sacred work, we find not only the true essence of Jewish tradition but also the path to a more just and compassionate world. Happy Pride Month, and may we all continue to be blessed with the strength to pursue justice, love, and equality for all!

A Spiritual Reflection on the Sanctity of Pride

Building love and equality in our world requires the recognition that God's image includes people of all genders and all orientations, and all sexual identities. This has been an evolving part of what it means to be part of a faith community, no question. But this is Pride Month, and a fine time for naming the inherent dignity of every human being, each one a beautiful refraction of divinity.

I learned the difference between tolerance and pride in a conversation I had once with a well-known rabbi in Jerusalem. In his Orthodox community, this rabbi was striving to build a bridge, so he convened a group of his students and a few of their family members, among which I was blessed to be counted. He spoke about the future for LGBTQ Jews in the Orthodox world, and I remember being in awe of his bravery for having the conversation within that context. For a long time, and still in many sectors of the Jewish world, there isn't a place created for this conversation. Many young people and many adults have suffered because their community has not affirmed their humanity. It really is that simple and that terrible, and not limited to Orthodoxy.

I remember this rabbi saying that he was trying to find a way to show tolerance. I recall someone in the crowd, who I knew was still in the closet but struggling because of their Orthodox upbringing, standing up. They said, "Rabbi, I appreciate you having this conversation, but I don't think we want to be tolerated. We want to be celebrated." This was their public coming out, and an incredibly important moment in my own Jewish journey to hear in person about the love that was possible between two men or two women, and to hear about it in terms of sanctity and celebration.

As part of Pride Month, we must ensure that we don't fall into the trap of using language like "tolerate" to talk about our children, our siblings, our parents, our family members, and our neighbors. In this moment, we are called to be part of the Jewish community's love of all our children and all our adults.

There are trailblazers from within the Jewish community, including Harvey Milk of blessed memory, and countless other leaders and modern faith leaders such as Rabbi Denise Eger, Rabbi Aaron Weininger, and Rabbi Steve Greenberg. In their respective worlds—the Conservative, Reform, and Orthodox worlds—they have shown the synthesis, even with struggle, of being who they each are in fullness.

While that burden is theirs, it is a test of our community's capacity for love to see what we can do with the model these brave teachers have shown.

This coming Sunday in New York, at the Pride Parade, there will be a wonderful gathering called "Jew York Pride." I'm especially proud that the UJA-Federation NY has co-sponsored this event historically with organizations like Eshel, which creates a beautiful tapestry for Orthodox gay Jews; JQY, which has done a lot of outreach in the Jewish queer youth world, especially but not only in the Orthodox world; Keshet, which is the leading national organization creating resources and programming and eye-opening conversations like the one that brought me into this work with its founder, my beloved friend Idit Klein; and countless other organizations, including Congregation Beit Simchat Torah, the largest queer synagogue in the world, located in Manhattan.

I focus on all this, friends, because we don't focus on it enough. This coming Sunday is Pride. I have been blessed to be there a few times. I cannot amplify the importance enough of the Jewish community affirming respect for our LGBTQ descendants and our LGBTQ ancestors. We have always sought to grow our circles of belonging and to evolve our consciousness to understand that the image of God looks like all of us and loves like all of us.

In this week's Torah portion, Shelach, there is a famous section where spies are sent to the Promised Land to scout it out, to see what it looks like, what's possible, what challenges lie ahead. When they return, they bring a critical incident report: this is what the land looks like, this is the topography, this is who lives there. They talk about the Nephilim, the fallen ones, saying, "We were grasshoppers in our own eyes, and so we must have seemed to them. (Num. 13:33)"

Let's talk about the deep wound this language signifies: when we looked at them, we felt so small, and so we must have looked small to them. This is where the problem really lived—in the spies not understanding that they were not small at all. They were the leaders of our people (Num. 13:2-3), each chosen for their capacity to stand tall, strong, and faithful. Their courage would inspire the community.

The two outliers of the group of spies, Joshua and Caleb, didn't deny the challenges ahead, but affirmed the capacity of the community to journey on with the now-famous promise, "We shall overcome. (Num 13:30)"

When our ancestors, these biblical pioneers and beautiful modern torchbearers we are blessed to know, stand up and say, "I see a world where all love is affirmed, where two human beings can build a holy life blessed by God and community, where pride is sanctified," we grow, as does Jewish tradition itself. We must all learn from them what it is to not see ourselves as grasshoppers. We're not too small to champion love. We're not too small to know that we're worthy of love.

We should never consider ourselves grasshoppers. It's appropriate and very human to have doubts and to be reflective, but when we do see ourselves in self-diminishing ways and then imagine that misperception in the eyes of others, we miss the obligation of every human being to recognize divine dignity, the core Torah truth that every human being is created in the image of God.

I remember the first time I officiated at a same-sex kiddushin, a same-sex Jewish wedding. It was new. I had never done it before. I stood under the chuppah and just did the traditional liturgy, replacing the language of groom and bride with bride and bride. It was so powerful, but not for the reasons I expected. I thought it would be powerful because it was something new, an expansion of holiness. That was true, but after that moment under the chuppah someone asked me afterward what it felt like, and my answer was the holiest feeling I know how to express: it felt like a wedding. It felt like love. It felt like God pouring through. It felt like two people who found each other in a world of billions. It felt like God was smiling.

Yes, tradition often has a long way to go, but isn't that part of God's process too? Isn't that part of what it means to be part of a divinely inspired trajectory of human beings just trying to make peace and life? Isn't it so beautiful to know that love is love? No one should feel like a grasshopper because every one of us has God's glowing heart embedded in our souls. The way we love is God's Love pouring out from us. The way our family members love, the way our neighbors love, is holy. If we don't see that, that's some work we need to do on ourselves because pride is the natural state loving and being loved.

So this Sunday, in honor of Pride, let us amplify the infinite beauties of the human heart: vibrant color, inner peace, and profound love.

Independence Day:
Relearning the Purpose of Freedom

Today is many things, including in America, the 4th of July. Let's ground this reflection on America's Independence Day in Torah and delve into the day's meaning.

In Parashat Korach we encounter a rebellion led by Korach, who recruits Datan and Aviram, who in turn enlist 250 leaders of the Israelites to stage a rebellion, not just against Moses and Aaron, but against the order established by God (Num. 16:1-3). This is significant because the authority Moses and Aaron wield is not their own, nor did they seek it. Moses tried to evade God's call, and Aaron was appointed as a spokesperson in a last-ditch effort to support Moses.

This is an important starting point because the power any leader wields is not their own. Ancient societies, and even modern ones like Japan with the idea of an emperor, believed leaders served in place of God. This was true in ancient Egypt as well. When God called Moses, God's language was said, "I will make you a god to Pharaoh, and Aaron will be your prophet, (Ex. 4:14-16)" underscoring that the prophet is the voice of God, just as the ruler was seen as the incarnation of God. Even the modern Catholic Church has a version of this in the role of the Pope.

But let us focus not on the authority of these leaders but the ritual by which they were tested. When Korach and the rebels challenged Aaron's place as High Priest, they were instructed to each take their fire pans and offer incense to God. The one whose offering was accepted would be affirmed as the rightful leader in a public spectacle (Num. 16: 16-17). Aaron's offering was accepted, while Korach's followers were consumed by divine fire (v. 35). The fire pans of the rebels were then melted down to cover the altar, serving as a lasting reminder of the rebellion (Num. 17:3).

Rabbi Charlie Schwarz, quoting Nechama Leibowitz (who was herself amplifying Ramban's commentary), explains that the physical transformation from fire-pans to altar-cover demonstrates that the holiness of these vessels did not originate from the actions of the sinners but rather symbolized the return of ritual order and the end of chaos.

Turning to today, American history is replete with chaotic chapters, often (at the time) seen as valorous and noble. My grandfather served in World War II, stationed in the Philippines, nearly part of a ground invasion of Japan before the U.S. dropped atomic bombs onto Hiroshima and Nagasaki in 1945. My sister, now a chaplain in the US Navy, continues this legacy of service. My pride in America is rooted in my family's service and the safe shores we found here generations earlier. But part of my civic responsibility includes acknowledging the complexity of American history and being part of writing the next and better chapter of our nation's story.

Today, the 4th of July marks the ratification of the Declaration of Independence in 1776. The founders of the United States were not demigods but humans improvising the best they could. Among their achievements was creating a nation without destroying it—a lesson in leadership worth emulating.

Korach and his followers sought power without pure intent. The incorporation of their fire pans into the altar reminds us all that part of service is to absorb the complex lessons of our history. As Americans, we must acknowledge the sins of our past, from the displacement and massacre of Indigenous peoples to the dehumanization of enslavement.

Judaism teaches that we do not erase sins but learn from them, striving to do better when presented with the same circumstances. The fire pans melted down and placed on the altar teach us never to forget.

Knowing our history is essential. In his book "American Creation," Joseph Ellis speaks about the founders' human flaws and their creative political foundation, which allowed for future leaders like Abraham Lincoln and Martin Luther King Jr. to further the nation's ideals as more modern founders in the great American experiment. Similarly, Jonathan Sarna's "American Judaism" highlights the contributions of American Jews to the United States' ongoing founding. The story of American Judaism is one of human potential and the ability to change history. Both books emphasize that the future is ours to create, reminding us that justice is a process, and authority must be wielded ethically.

As we reflect on the 4th of July, we must remember that no place is perfect or fully complete. The mistakes of the past are integral to the lessons we need to serve. The fire pans of Korach remind us to absorb and learn from our history, moving the needle toward justice and real freedom.

The 4th of July is not just a date in 1776; it is today. The sacrifices of our ancestors have brought us here. So: what are we willing to contribute in this moment of history so that our children will be blessed to say the same?

Shiva Assar BeTammuz After October 7:
Breached Walls and The End of Exile

Today is a complicated day. Not only has it been 291 days since October 7th, but today is also Shiva Assar BeTammuz, the 17th day of the Hebrew month of Tammuz. This minor fast day carries enormous significance as it marks the beginning of the three weeks leading up to Tisha B'Av, ones of the saddest days on the Jewish calendar. Tisha B'Av stood alone as the saddest day until Yom HaShoah was added, and now, October 7th will likely be counted among these tragic days for its own very significant and obvious reasons.

On the 17th of Tammuz, tradition tells us that Moshe broke the tablets when he saw the Israelites worshipping a golden calf. During the Siege of Jerusalem by the Babylonians, we were forced to stop offering sacrifices. According to tradition, a foreigner burned a Torah, an idol was placed in the Jerusalem Temple, and in 69 CE, just before the Temple was destroyed in 70 CE, the walls of Jerusalem were breached. These are very sad days, and this is a sad period of time. Some people refrain from shaving, doing laundry, or buying new things during these three weeks leading up to Tisha B'Av. The fast begins in the morning and ends in the evening, and while not everyone observes it, those who do engage in specific prayers and rituals that reflect the somber nature of the day.

What makes this year's Shiva Assar BeTammuz especially poignant is the breaching of the walls of our holy place, evoking our lived experience of October 7th. On that day, terrorists breached our world with bulldozers and weapons, marking a failure of Israel's Defense Forces and the government in Israel. It's a very intense thing to live through the ritual commemoration of an ancient version of what that represented. While it's not historically accurate to conflate two different times, trauma does trigger trauma. As I stand here in my imagination on Kibbutz Kfar Aza in the south of Israel, where I journeyed with elected officials from Westchester two months after October 7th, I recall the vivid and painful memories of what I witnessed.

Our ancient rituals on Shiva Assar BeTammuz are ways of keeping history alive so we can learn from it, grieve healthily, and grow. Walking through Kibbutz Kfar Aza, I see the markings on the buildings left by the terrorists and the hole in the fence where they breached the walls. Shiva Assar BeTammuz and the three weeks that follow are about seeing what a breach in those walls represents.

We are reeling 291 days later, not only because of the physical breaches and assaults but also because of the deep emotional and communal wounds. The founding of the state of Israel in 1948 was meant to end such stories of exile and vulnerability, but history has shown us otherwise. On days like today, we must remember the lessons of our ancestors and acknowledge that the threat of breaching walls and dehumanization still exists. It's hard to comprehend how anyone could intend the atrocities committed on October 7th, but we do a disservice to our ancestors if we deny the existence of evil in the world.

As I stand here in my imagination, both in Kibbutz Kfar Aza and Ancient Jerusalem, I'm reminded of the importance of history. Shiva Assar BeTammuz is not just about mourning; it's about actively remembering and learning from our past. The breaching of the walls of Jerusalem is echoed in the breaches of October 7th. Our ancestors' resilience and strength must inspire us to protect our future.
Today, we face our history honestly and with heart. We carry the broken heart of our people within us, and while Shiva Assar BeTammuz may be a minor fast day, there's nothing minor about its lessons. As we remember, we also honor the extraordinary heroism and resilience of our sisters and brothers in Israel. We recognize the necessity of protecting ourselves and learning from our history.

May the Exile end, and may our children and grandparents come home. May we amplify our calls for justice and safety until all our loved ones are home. We are the people who remember, heal, and grow. May we continue to be authentic descendants and worthy ancestors, carrying our people's history and resilience forward.

Grief and Hope on Shabbat Chazon

As we approach Tisha B'Av, one of the saddest days on the Jewish calendar, we enter a period of deep reflection and mourning. This day commemorates numerous tragedies in Jewish history, most notably the destruction of the two Temples in Jerusalem, first in 586 BCE and then in 70 CE. The days leading up to Tisha B'Av, known as the "Nine Days," immerse us in a unique form of grief, what experts might call "anticipatory grief."

Let us first consider the broader concept. We are in a time that not only leads into Tisha B'Av but is also framed by this special Shabbat, known as Shabbat Chazon, the "Shabbat of Vision." It takes its name from the opening words of the Haftarah, which portrays a vision of Jerusalem destroyed and the Jewish People in Exile. This Shabbat is a moment of profound sadness, a time when we confront the stark reality of loss and devastation.

Yet, even in this somber period, we find profound wisdom in our tradition. Peter Capaldi, the actor who played Doctor Who, once said in the face of great loss, "Things end, and that's always sad. But things begin again, and that's always happy." This resonates deeply with the message of Shabbat Chazon and the lead-up to Tisha B'Av. Yes, it is a sad time. But within our tradition, there is also a vision of renewal—a belief that out of the ashes, something new can emerge. If Shabbat Chazon is here, we know Shabbat Nachamu, a Shabbat of Comfort, is on the horizon.

We are currently living through a time of great pain, not only in remembering past tragedies but also in witnessing ongoing suffering in our world. The pain of those who are displaced, the heartbreak of families torn apart—these are the modern-day echoes of the grief we commemorate on Tisha B'Av.

Jewish wisdom navigates grief through a series of stages. In a more typical loss, Jewish tradition guides us through the immediate mourning rituals, beginning with the burial, moving into Shiva (the first seven days of mourning), then to Sheloshim (the first 30 days), and for the loss of a parent, an extended period of eleven months. Each stage gradually ritually releases us from the intense grip of grief, offering a pathway to healing.

But Tisha B'Av is different. The grief here is anticipatory, layered, and complex. We journey from the three weeks of mourning, to the more intense nine days, and finally to the singular day of Tisha B'Av, where the culmination of our collective sorrow is expressed. This model of anticipatory grief, allows us to prepare for loss, a concept that might seem strange at first but is deeply embedded in our tradition.

The four hallmarks of anticipatory grief (I am grateful here to Rabbi Melanie Levav for her insights on this) - accepting the inevitability of death, feeling concern for the dying, rehearsing the death, and imagining the future—are all present in our approach to Tisha B'Av. Moshe, in Parashat Devarim (which we read every year on Shabbat Chazon), models this acceptance as he acknowledges his own impending death and yet offers a vision for the future of his people. This Shabbat invites us to envision a future even as we confront the painful realities of the present.

As we mark the 308th day since October 7th, a day that brought so much pain to our People, Am Yisrael, we are reminded of the ongoing struggles that continue to affect us. The weight of these tragedies is heavy, but our tradition compels us to look beyond the sorrow, to imagine a future that is brighter and more hopeful. As Elie Wiesel poignantly wrote,

> "When the world ceases giving Jews reason for hope, Jews invent new reasons for hope."

So, as we enter Shabbat Chazon and approach Tisha B'Av, let us fully engage with our grief, following the path laid out by our tradition. But let us also dare to envision a future that transcends the darkness of the present. This is the true power of our faith—the ability to hold onto hope, even in the most challenging times.

Burned but Unbroken: The Day After Tisha Be'Av

The day after Tisha B'Av is an emotional bridge. Yesterday was a hard day for many of us, a day designed in our tradition to hold the deep well of Jewish sorrow. It's not that the sadness suddenly disappears, but we have been given the gift of a day to contain it. That gives us permission, maybe even the responsibility, to start cultivating joy again, to remind ourselves of the life force that still pulses through and within us as individuals, and as Am Yisrael.

It's important to pause, take a breath, and reflect. Tradition tells us that the fires which burned our Temple in 70 CE still smoldered the next day—today. So, while we step into the future, we are not free from the pain of Tisha B'Av just yet. But here's the wisdom of our tradition: we hold the pain, but we are also called to choose life.

This week's Torah portion, Va'Etchanan, speaks directly to this delicate balance. Moses, knowing he won't enter the Promised Land, pours his heart into his final words. He stands before us with a sense of urgency, reminding us to cling to God, to hold fast to the holiness that sustains life, even in the face of loss.

One verse stands out:

> "V'atem hadvekim b'Hashem Elokeichem chayim kulchem hayom"—"But you who hold fast to God, you are all alive today. (Deut. 4:4)"

This is not encouragement to enhance life through spirituality, but rather a fierce call to action. To hold fast to God is like grabbing onto a lifeline in the middle of a stormy sea. Life can feel like chaos swirling around us, and all we can do is grab hold of the thread of divinity that grounds us, that keeps us afloat.

That lifeline, friends, is Torah. Torah is our anchor, our way to live fully even as we navigate pain. Moses knew he wouldn't be with the people forever, but he offered them a gift—a tradition that can sustain us in every storm. Whether we are in grief, in joy, or in the complicated space between, Torah pulls us back to life, back to purpose.

Today, as we emerge from the sorrow of Tisha B'Av, let us remember that our task is not to forget the pain, but to integrate it. Life doesn't wait for us to feel fully ready. Life, with its beauty and its brokenness, is here, right now. And we are alive today. That means we have work to do. We have the responsibility to bring light into the world, to offer prayers for healing, to hold each other close in the spirit of love.

So as we transition from sorrow to hope, let's cling to the lifeline of Torah, and through that connection, send strength and prayers to those who are still in darkness. We are a people who survive by holding tight to life, and in doing so, we bring healing and hope into the world. May this be our mission today and always.

Accountability and Comfort
(Va'Etchanan / Shabbat Nachamu)

As we turn to the Torah, we reflect on the powerful transitions we witness in our tradition. Last Shabbat was Shabbat Chazon, the Shabbat of Vision, where the prophet Isaiah foresees the destruction of Jerusalem (Is. 1:1-27). We read that haftarah as we approach Tisha B'Av, the day commemorating the destruction of the Temple. This past Tuesday marked Tisha B'Av itself—a day of profound mourning and reflection.

But tonight, we enter Shabbat Nachamu, the Shabbat of Comfort. After the devastation, after the tears, comes a promise of consolation. This time Isaiah speaks to our hearts, to the very heart of Jerusalem:

> "Nachamu, Nachamu Ami—Be comforted, be comforted, My people. (Is. 40:1)"

Yet comfort in these times feels complicated. Our hearts are heavy, not only with the weight of history but with the realities of our present. We pray fervently for the safety of our People, and we watch, sometimes with pride, sometimes with shame, as we navigate the complexities of building a homeland. Recently, we witnessed a horrifying act of violence as Jewish extremists attacked a Palestinian town. It's a dark stain on our community, but what separates us from those who perpetuate hatred is our insistence on accountability. We demand justice because we are a people committed to Torah, to the idea that our actions have consequences.

This week, in Parshat Va'etchanan, Moses reminds the people of this very truth. As they prepare to enter the Promised Land, he warns them that how they conduct themselves matters, that the world is watching.

> "[Your adherence to God's commands] will be proof of your wisdom and discernment to other peoples, who on hearing of all these laws will say, 'Surely, that great nation is a wise and discerning people.' ... But take utmost care and watch yourselves scrupulously, so that you do not forget the things that you saw with your own eyes and so that they do not fade from your mind as long as you live. ... For your own sake, therefore, be most careful. (Deut. 4: 6, 9, 15)"

Moses, who is denied entry into the land, implores the people to honor the gift they are about to receive. To be a Jew means that the eyes of history are always upon us. While we cannot prevent Antisemitism through our right behavior, we can ensure that we hold ourselves accountable to the highest standards of our tradition.

And accountability itself is a form of comfort. Judaism never presumes we are perfect; it understands that we will make mistakes. What matters is how we respond to those mistakes—how we engage in teshuvah, in return and repentance. These seven weeks between Tisha B'Av and Rosh Hashanah are a time for reflection and for lifting the world higher. That too is comfort: knowing that we have the power to do better, to be better, to heal our world, one step at a time.

There are many forms of comfort we seek. We take comfort in our ability to rebuild and perfect our home, in knowing that the work of healing is ongoing. We take comfort in the belief that our family, our people, will return home. Most of all, we take comfort in the knowledge that we can create the world we need, that we can make choices today that will echo into the future.

As we welcome Shabbat Nachamu, let us open our hearts to the possibilities of comfort—comfort we must create with our own hands and our own choices. There are big decisions ahead of us: decisions about leadership, about the future of our beloved Israel, about how we show up for our students, our communities, and ourselves. May all of our choices be a comfort to Moses, our ancient teacher, and to the precious generations yet to come.

Let us raise our voices in song, in prayer, and in hope. May the negotiations bear fruit. May our family come home. May this Shabbat truly be a Shabbat of comfort for our people, so that we can begin the long work of healing.

And may we, one day, know peace.

Memory and Kindness:
Reflections on 9/11 and Ki Teitzei

On the 23rd anniversary of 9/11, we find ourselves revisiting memories that have shaped our world. Each of us has different memories of where we were on that day. It is crucial to pause and share these moments, to offer them up as acts of remembrance and healing. I invite you, friends, to share your own reflections, to bring forth blessings from your memory in this space. In doing so, we connect our personal histories to the collective, reminding us that memory itself is sacred.

I remember being a fifth-year rabbinical student at the Jewish Theological Seminary. All the leaders were away, and we, the senior students, found ourselves unexpectedly tasked with guiding the community through the shock of that day. We didn't know what to do, but we knew we needed to gather people together. I vividly recall the disbelief when I heard the news, a clear blue Tuesday morning, the kind of day where you can't imagine such devastation unfolding. Yet it did, and the world as we knew it shifted.

As I raced back to the Seminary after hearing the second tower had been hit, I remember Rabbi Alan Kensky, our dean at the time, sharing a story that anchored us: in moments of terror, we continue to learn Torah, to hold on to who we are. And even though the moment defied understanding, we leaned into our tradition as a source of stability.

This week's Torah portion, Ki Teitzei, calls us into memory. It lists moments of attack and survival, challenging us to confront who we've been and how we respond. Theologian Judith Plaskow writes that memory brings with it an obligation to ethical discernment: we must decide which memories to affirm and which to transform. In Ki Teitzei, we are commanded to blot out the memory of Amalek, yet also to remember Amalek's cruelty. How do we do both?

On 9/11, the cruelty was clear. But what followed in the immediate aftermath was something else entirely. We saw glimpses of kindness, of gentleness, of a shared patriotism rooted not in division, but in our collective pain. People looked out for each other. Strangers comforted strangers. We didn't ask who voted how; we simply asked, "Are you okay?"

It's this kindness that I urge us to remember today. Not the anger or the later geopolitics, but the tender hearts we carried in the days following the attack. We honored first responders. We checked in on neighbors. We saw each other as human first.

Ki Teitzei reminds us that memory can both anchor and transform us. As we remember those we lost and the unity we experienced, let's ask ourselves: who were we then, and who do we want to be now? With the gift of today, how do we build a better tomorrow? Let us bless each other with gentleness, with radical compassion, and with the understanding that life is precious—so what will we do with it?

Claim Life. Today.
(Rosh HaShannah / Nitzavim)

The High Holidays invite us to a radical reckoning with ourselves and the world. They call us to show up, to fill the space we were meant to fill, and to live as fully as we were created to live.

On the cusp of a New Year, we stand before God with trembling Jewish hearts, broken and bruised after a year of trauma. How can we imagine rebecoming whole in a world that has provided no easy answers and in a moment that is distinguished from the last one only by the calendar. And, if we can find a breath, we might even remember to ask ourselves: what do we need?

We'd like many things, but what do we truly need? Courage. The courage to live today as if it matters, because it does.

"Give us courage." That's how the High Holiday prayer *Hayom* begins. And when we sing it, there's a sacred echo, as every voice carries the weight of these words, as if we are saying aloud what we've always known but struggled to admit. It's the bold declaration of who we truly are. Rosh Hashanah, the birthday of the Universe, reminds us that every day is our birthday, and Jewish tradition in this way makes a stunning claim—that God's deepest care is not just for one tribe, one nation, but for all of existence. Every blade of grass, every animal, every human being is precious.

This reflection ties into this week's Parasha, Nitzavim. The word "hayom"—today—appears five times in the first six verses. Moshe, knowing it is his last day on Earth, tells us: *you're here today.* All of you. From the woodchopper to the water-drawer, every soul is present. "Don't miss today," he seems to whisper, "because it's all we have." Five times, he pleads with us, reminding us not to let the weight of life make us forget the beauty of it.

As we approach this unreal Rosh Hashanah, this idea is magnified. What do we need to live fully, to be present, even in this day? *Courage.* And as we move into this sacred season, we ask God for three things: courage, blessing, and the strength to defy the world and be our full size as Jews. History's weight and current anti-Jewish hate can shrink us, but we were created to stand tall, to do good, to lift each other up, as human beings, and as Jews.

I feel this powerfully when I lead the prayers. As the melodies rise, I am often in tears. The enormity of life, the pain, the responsibility, the love—it's overwhelming. But it's also the greatest gift. And so, I ask God, in these aching, intense Days of Awe: *help us live. Give us life. Help us claim it with everything we have.* Remind us to demand what we need, not just for ourselves, but for our beleaguered, beautiful People. And one day, when we have our feet beneath us again, for the whole world.

As we walk through the world, we pass other people. Some look fine; some look as though the weight of the world is crushing them. We should pray for each one, because none of us should bear this weight alone. God, let us remember that our power is in seeking peace, in showing up for each other, and in not waiting for tomorrow. And if that remains true in Rosh HaShannah's broad vista of all of existence, then let us remember to include, nay, prioritize, Am Yisrael in our prayers this year.

Today is the day. *Hayom*—right now, we have the chance to promise ourselves life once again. May we – Am Yisrael – rise once again to the fullness of who we are, the image of God within us, with full human dignity, and may we be blessed to see it in each other. Let's not wait, friends. Let's start now. We deserve life. All of us do.

Sing it with me: *hayom.* Today is the day. Don't wait. Not even for Rosh Hashanah.

Claim life. Today.

We Are Bigger than This Moment:
Jewish Holidays are Jewish Defiance

In 1973, Elie Wiesel delivered a talk entitled *Against Despair*, which has gripped me deeply for the last 11 months. Every time I revisit it, I feel thunderstruck. Wiesel's words are not just useful—they are transformative. Prescient even. Somehow, he knew we'd need his fiery, hard-won wisdom this holiday season. (Or perhaps, maybe the world has changed less than we'd thought in the fifty years since he bequeathed us this message.)

Wiesel writes about the fragility and courage required to live and lead as Jews, no matter our circumstance. His unceasing, creative thinking after unspeakable trauma—ensuring that the rich spiritual tradition he inherited would continue to thrive—has always been deeply inspiring. His work translated the lessons of genocide into a call for justice, for everyone, while never abandoning the deep tribal connection to his people nor remaining silent when the State Israel was under threat.

Enemies of the Jews have always sought to steal Jewish time by attacking us on our holiest days, to *"turn the Jewish past against the Jews."* Wiesel points out that the Babi Yar massacres of 1941 happened on Yom Kippur. But how many of us knew that? That even the most engaged and historically-minded of us don't often know this that tells us that Yom Kippur is bigger than Babi Yar. Yom Kippur is bigger than the Yom Kippur War. Our sacred calendar itself declares to the world – and reminds every Jew: No one has the right to tell us when to be joyful or how to feel on our holy days.

October 7th is now part of our history, another moment when enemies tried to steal Jewish time by desecrating our homeland and the holy day of Simchat Torah. But I challenge us to ask: How big is Simchat Torah to us? Is it small enough that someone can overpower it, or is it bigger than anything thrown at us? I don't often speak in terms of "us and them," but I find myself increasingly doing so in recent months. This is a moment for tribal reflection. Simchat Torah is ours—bigger than any force that could come against us. We are bigger than that.

Wiesel offers two vignettes that pierce the soul. In one, Jews pressed together in a train to their deaths realized it was Simchat Torah. Someone had smuggled in a small Sefer Torah, and they began singing, swaying, and celebrating. In another, within a concentration camp barrack, they had no Sefer Torah, so:

An old man - was he really old? The word had no meaning there - noticed a young boy - who was so old, so old - standing there looking on and dreaming. "Do you remember what you learned in *heder*?" asked the man. "Yes, I do," replied the boy. "Really?" said the man, "you really remember *Shma Yisrael*?" "I remember much more," said the boy. "*Shma Yisrael* is enough," said the man. And he lifted the boy, clasped him in arms, and began dancing with him - as though he were the Torah. And all joined in. They all sang and danced and cried. They wept, but they sang with fervor - never before had Jews celebrated Simchat Torah with such fervor.

These stories embody what it means to face despair as a Jew—not by ignoring it, but by transforming it into hope. We cannot allow others to decide when we will be joyous or when we will mourn. In Wiesel's words,

We had to rejoice...and let the world know that Jews can sublimate pain and agony, and draw new reasons for hope from despair.

Faced with despair, Wiesel taught that we have three choices: resignation, delusion, or the most difficult and beautiful—facing it head-on as Jews.

This is not about ignoring the pain.

It's about resisting despair in our own way, by reclaiming our time, our joy, and our rituals.

I bless us to find our way back to dancing, to singing with fervor. We are bigger than this moment, no matter how heavy it feels. *We will dance again.* Wiesel taught us that, and I pray we all find that strength.

Even and especially now.

Amen.

The Counterbalance of the Holidays

In every historic moment of crisis, Am Yisrael, the Jewish People, responds—not passively, but with strength and resilience. The world has always been unsteady; if you're a student of history, you know this truth. But today, technology heightens that unsteadiness. We watch, in real-time, missiles intercepted over Tel Aviv—a place where my sister and her family live, along with countless others. Tel Aviv, that city of vibrant Jewish life, a symbol of new beginnings built on the old. Even its name speaks to this—"Tel," an archaeological mound, layered with history; "Aviv," spring, signaling rebirth. (This name is, in turn, a Hebrew adaptation of Herzl's 1902 utopian novel envisioning a Jewish State, "*Altneuland*," or "*Old New Land*.")

As we approach the holidays, the calendar reminds us: Time continues. We are here, enduring. The news might threaten to overwhelm us, but the rhythm of our sacred days offers a counterbalance. We don't get to choose whether or not these days arrive, and that, in itself, is a gift. The shofar will blow, even in a world ravaged by war and fear. Our rituals persist, and with them, we remind ourselves that we are still here.

Throughout our history, through every trial, we have pulsed with the lifeblood of our People. Our response—spiritual, emotional, and fierce—reminds us that we are not small. We are larger than this moment. Our work, whether it's protecting students from antisemitism or aiding Holocaust survivors, is part of an eternal mission. We endure. *Am Yisrael Chai!* This is no small thing, and neither are we.

Tomorrow is never promised, but today—*hayom*—is here. In the opening verses of this week's Torah portion, Nitzavim, Moses implores us to choose life, to recognize that every day we stand at the crossroads of blessing and curse. And the choice is always ours: Will we live fully? Will we commit ourselves to reflection, repair, and strengthening our bonds with each other, with our past, and with our future?

The High Holidays invite us to return—to God, to ourselves, to each other. And as we scream at the heavens on Yom Kippur, we are not making threats. We are declaring our presence, our resolve. We are still here. And then, as Sukkot arrives, we build our fragile huts, inviting our ancestors to join us once more. We dance with Torah in hand, not because the world has made it easy, but because Torah demands it of us. Torah teaches us to choose life, to grip onto its teachings, and never let go.

This is our sacred mandate: to live fully, to choose life, again and again. We are witnesses to life itself, and by our very presence, we declare that we will endure.

Am. Yisrael. Chai!

AFTERWORD

One People, One Heart:
The Day After One Year Later

Yesterday's history is the Torah we live through; today's Torah is the one we write with our lives, with our fierce determination to keep going.

The Global Jewish People has been there through every major chapter of Jewish history in the last century—helping birth the State of Israel, supporting Jews arriving in America, lifting up communities through the pandemic, and showing up on the ground for Ukraine. And now, post-October 7th, we continue to be there for Israel, over and over again.

But yesterday, watching my friend Eric Goldstein, CEO of UJA-Federation of New York, standing at Nova at Kibbutz Re'im—where our hearts were torn open—it struck me deeply. We are survivors, all of us. The dancers, the singers, the leaders—they are our rabbis today. Their survival is sacred. No, it's not the same as those who survived the Shoah, but the reverence we give them is profoundly resonant.

Friends, as we look forward to Yom Kippur, we remember how to count our days. "Teach us to number our days, so we may attain a heart of wisdom. (Ps. 90:12)" These days between Rosh Hashanah and Yom Kippur are so much more than days of repentance—they are days of repair, days of return, days of rising higher and higher.

Yesterday, I saw a community alive, even in the face of deep grief. I saw the strength of New York's Jewish community, the love that was on full display, the beauty of interfaith unity, and the music of our youth, from high school students to college a cappella groups, lifting us all. And I was reminded again that we know how to mark time. We know how to cherish every minute.

Are we ready to make every day count? Are we ready to fight for our dignity, our bodies, and our family in Israel? Our history has taught us that the fight never truly ends. But every day, we have a choice to rise, to act, to love, to make a difference.

Let this be a year of rebuilding, of health, of strength, and of hope. Let us pray for it, and then let's do everything in our power to make it so. Together, let's send our hearts eastward, to Israel, where we are Lev Echad, Am Echad - One People, with One Heart.

Deep breath. Let's begin again.

Rabbi Menachem Creditor serves as the Pearl and Ira Meyer Scholar in Residence at UJA-Federation New York and was the founder of Rabbis Against Gun Violence. An acclaimed author, scholar, and speaker with over 5 million views of his online videos and essays, he was named by Newsweek as one of the fifty most influential rabbis in America. His numerous books and 6 albums of original music include the global anthem "*Olam Chesed Yibaneh*" and the COVID-era 2-volume anthology "*When We Turned Within.*" He and his wife Neshama Carlebach live in New York, where they are raising their five children.